S.H.O.R.E.

The Ultimate Descent

Asma Jan Muhammad

In case you are wondering why the title has periods within, it is a mnemonic of the names of the main characters of the book.

S(Sheriff).H(Harry).O(Olive).R(Rob).Ellis(Ellis);

something to make readers remember them easily ☺.

Happy reading!

To all the resilient souls who never cease to amaze this world with their ambition and passion.

Table of Contents

Prologue

June 05, 2021, the date Olive and her team members would not forget for the rest of their life. After years of lobbying and dissent against the authoritarian Rob, the supreme council of the Board had conceded to their demands and decided to hold fresh elections on that very day to select the governing body of the Club—its international working platform. Olive, leader of the Like-Minded, was the favorite to win against her Unionist counterpart, Rob. However, nothing could be taken for granted given the Club's inter-organizational political dynamics.

The customary 6:30 a.m. alarm was inconsequential; Olive was already awake. Being an early bird, she was used to getting up early; today, though, it was more due to nervous excitement. Despite the assurances from the Club's members, she knew how fatal it would be to assume favorable results beforehand. It was the perfect case of *it is not over until it is over.* Deep in her thoughts, Olive went to her apartment's balcony to enjoy the sunrise while sipping away the freshly-brewed Cuban coffee. The morning breeze and the aroma of strong coffee were the only things that could relax her mind.

Midtown Houston was getting ready to welcome the last day of the week. People were walking in the parks and on the pathways; some were walking their pets. Traffic was less than normal, more so because of the summer vacations. The usual vibrancy of the area was nonexistent. But Olive liked it this way. Not a big fan of the hustle and bustle, she has always enjoyed the early morning bird's-eye view of the neighborhood. It has a soothing effect on her and was her antidote to all the stress and anxiety—something she has had a lot in the recent past.

Olive was a team leader for internal audit in a national pharmaceutical company. The recent Pandemic and subsequent changes in the work settings had drained a lot out of her and her team. The company, a producer of life-saving drugs, was allowed to operate but with a limited workforce at the facility. Initially, they had to work in shifts to comply with the restrictions. However, hell seemed to break loose when the complete lockdown was imposed. Ensuring the veracity of data received, coordinating with the production team about their requirements, and allocating the resources for the coming months proved cumbersome. Communication proficiency while working from home was not as efficient as working on-site. It seemed everyone was lost. Thinking about those days still gave Olive jitters. Unlike Mathew, she was relieved when offices reopened to full attendance. Even on those tiring work-from-home days, the balcony provided her with much-needed comfort, allowing Olive to mentally switch on and off to maintain the balance between professional and personal lives.

"Honey, if you are already up, can you please turn off the alarm," Mathew, Olive's husband, called from behind.

"Ohh… I am so sorry. Here, done," she replied apologetically. "By the way, someone told me yesterday that he needed to get to his office early, and in case you are wondering, it is 6:40 a.m. now," Olive continued, taking a jibe at her sleepy husband.

Mathew, who was clearly not in the mood to leave his cozy bed, got up thinking about the early morning meeting he had scheduled for today. Heading toward the restroom, he observed restlessness in Olive.

"Are you OK? You are looking a bit tense; is something bothering you?"

"No, I am perfectly fine. Just thinking about the voting," Olive replied.

"There is no need to worry about something you can't control; it will reflect badly on you. Think positively. Getting the supreme council to conduct fresh elections is a win in itself, isn't it? Who would have thought the *irreplaceable* Rob would be challenged, and that too by a *meek young lady*? Your confidence is your strength; don't lose it when you need it the most.

"Secondly, the majority have given you their word; why worry now? They are all educated adults. Seriously, look at them; they are all certified accountants and represent the educational elite of our country. Plus, they all are professionals and have been making important decisions for their respective companies; certainly, they can make a sensible choice for the betterment of their club. It's Friday; still, two days are left; don't spoil your weekend for that." Mathew tried his best to brighten the mood of his lovely wife.

"That's what I am afraid of, Mat. Rob knows that I have the backing of the majority and will do anything to protect his chairmanship. He will not die wondering!"

Chapter One: The Club

The Board prides itself in being the mother institute of all the qualified accountants in the country, the alma mater. It was founded by the government to provide on-job training to young and aspiring auditors and financial planners to cater to the industrial need for a smooth supply of competent professionals in the field. Consequently, its founding members, trainers, and supervisors created a strong bond with the powerful industrialists. The appreciation and respect afforded the organization a great opportunity to spread its influence. Soon, it evolved into an educational system, devising courses and issuing certifications. The market's recognition garnered acknowledgment among the masses, who started to view it as a source of secured and high-earning jobs. Getting a certificate from the Board became the dream of many teenagers in this jobs-starved country.

The hype meant that local colleges and private tutors started making a beeline for registration. Despite its huge popularity, the Board's policy was simple: they would only develop the courses, conduct the exams, and issue the certificate; preparation was the students' responsibility. With only guidelines and a list of books available to them, there was uncertainty among the pupils on how to go about things. The lure of getting a well-recognized accounting certification was too tempting, but so was the risk of the unknown. All the educational institutions and tutors entered the market, eyeing that gap to cash in. They all promised to provide the best reading material and the most qualified professors to help their students score heavily in the exams. With a competitive job market and an uncertain future looming, many took the bait.

Though the chain looked simple and logical: an educational body with affiliated institutions imparting accounting and financial education, there was more than what met the eye. Beneath the waterline existed a dirty nexus between the colleges and the Board. They colluded, for their own interest, to keep a cap on the passing percentage of the students to make the most out of them. All this was done in the name of producing quality products and not allowing the market to reach the saturation point. With no rules and regulations overseeing the working of the Board, many serving members partnered with the management of the institutes to make some easy money.

The Board's prime objective was to train accounts and finance professionals and to appraise them about internationally recognized accounting principles. It supervised their work and recognized them through certifications. The document provided a wealth of opportunities for the trainees, opening the doors of higher management to them. Not long after, the same apprentices, who had benefited from the system, started their own tax and auditing consultancy services. It was the payback time. Here again, the Board members conspired with the accounting services providers and created an entry barrier for the others, whom they felt were outsiders.

Despite being one of the industry's most prestigious and influential working bodies, the Board was not functioning professionally. After managing the affairs for some time, the government left its management to the experts, hoping they would be able to run it better. However, the members devised a constitution that allowed only *volunteers* to get elected as directors. They were either the owners of accounting colleges or auditing firms; becoming a director only served them an opportunity to advance their personal interests even further. In simpler terms, it allowed them to legalize all their wrongdoings.

Therefore, the Board, which was created to ensure the ethical implementation of accounting standards and laws, became the harbinger of financial corruption in the country. It provided cover for the illicit practices of corrupt industrialists and politicians, giving them a clean sheet to keep working. In a developing country, seeped in income disparity and very few opportunities for the common person, it broadened the gulf between the elite and the middle class.

Meanwhile, some of the senior members of the Board, who had left the country disheartened by the corruption, started raising their voices against the malpractices of their ex-colleagues. As a token of giving back to society in their mother country, they decided to unite and protest collectively. For this purpose, they created a platform, the Club. The idea was to bring all the disgruntled accountants living outside the country under one roof and launch a strong opposition. Since the majority of the diaspora lived in the United States, Houston was chosen as the headquarters, with James as the first president of the Club. Social media accounts were created to reach as many people as possible and create awareness.

James had lived in the U.S. for more than thirty years and was loved by the locals equally as by his compatriots living in the area. He had served in major multinationals and was known for his strict principles and ethics. For the professionals worried about the negative image of their country due to the Board's wrongdoings, James was the obvious choice. He offered in-depth knowledge of the organization and a spotless career.

News about the formation of the Club spread instantly among the students and junior members of the Board. As the membership swelled, the team found it appropriate to form a working committee that would work exclusively to communicate with the members and arrange networking events. Later, that working committee transformed into a board of directors, supervising all the work. They were assisted by different teams working in their areas. For transparency, founding members decided to give every team the power to vote for the board of directors and the president. This way, they wanted to keep everyone involved in check, preventing any misuse of power. Initially, there were five teams covering Texas; they were led by Rob, Sheriff, Ellis, Harry, and Paul. The board of directors includes Henry, Daniel, Thomas, and Michael. The Club team worked tirelessly and managed to create a name for themselves; people from the accounting and finance field internationally started to take them seriously. The International Association of Accountants (IAAC) even sent a letter to the Board, asking for clarification. It was worried about the level of irregularities in one of its associated organizations.

The Club's popularity got everyone on the Board alarmed. They were not expecting such a strong dissenting voice, and that too from their ex-colleagues. Aron, the president of the Board, called a meeting to discuss the matter. They all were clearly disturbed by the progress the Club was making.

"Gentlemen, this Club is becoming more than a nuisance now. Something needs to be done, and fast," Aron was clear in his opening remarks to other directors.

They all nodded.

"I know a person who is very active in the Club. His name is Sheriff; we both worked in the same audit firm during our internship. If you guys agree, I can talk to him to gain some insight into their working. Secondly, if my memory serves me right, Sheriff was a man who only served his interests. If you know what it means," Joshua said with a mischievous grin.

"So you are proposing to buy one of the persons of the Club? Will it work? What if he informs his people it will open a new Pandora's box for us," Aron was visibly not impressed.

"There is no harm in trying. And initially, I will talk to him as a batchmate and try to keep our conversation generic. Things are bad as they are; don't think they can get worse," Joshua especially emphasized in the later part.

"I second Joshua. Let us give it a shot, and if it doesn't work out, we will back out. If Sheriff tries to play smart, we will discredit everything, saying that it was only between the two batchmates and the Board has nothing to do with that," Rutherford chimed in.

With Rutherford behind his back, Joshua looked at other directors to say *do you have anything better to propose.* As no other board member outrightly opposed the idea, Aron reluctantly agreed for Joshua to communicate with Sheriff. However, he cautioned him to be extra careful. He was annoyed that Johusa took the limelight during the meeting. Bowing down to an adversary during such an important meeting was the last thing Aron had wanted, but he didn't have a better alternate.

***

Early on a Sunday morning, the Sheriff's mobile buzzed. It was a text message from an unknown number.

"Hey, Sheriff, old buddy. This is Joshua; hope you remember me. I am in Houston for a week. Can we catch up? Reply when free. Thanks."

A smile spread across Sheriff's face as he read the message. Joshua was his best mate during the internship. Even during the most tiring days, Joshua would come up with something funny to brighten their mood. They had spent plenty of nights together, preparing for their exams.

"Hello, Joshua. Where have you been? Long time no see, mate! I am always free for you; just let me know the location and time. Looking forward to meeting you."

"Tonight, 8 p.m., Navy Blue."

"Perfect, done."

Later that night, both met as per the schedule.

"Josh, how are you, man? You have grown old? By the way, how did you get my number?" Sheriff bombarded his friend with a number of questions. He was still in a state of disbelief that they were meeting after more than a decade.

"Sheriff, I have my connections," Joshua said with his famous sly grin. "Everything was fine till you guys decided to start that club. It is graying my hair," he complained.

"Hahaha. Then you better stop all this nonsense and for once practice what you preach; follow the standards," Sheriff retorted.

"OK, OK…, Sheriff, I am not here to hear all this stuff. I am here for the seafood and to meet with my friend, to relive some of our memories. Hope you don't mind." Saying that Joshua raised both his hands in mock surrender.

"You will never change, Josh."

After that meeting, Joshua and Sheriff started exchanging messages frequently. For Sheriff, it was about reuniting with the old friend; however, Joshua was trying to make use of Sheriff's influence to find out more about the Club.

One night, Sheriff sounded disturbed. Upon enquiry, he informed Joshua that the Club would be conducting president's elections soon.

"Though I want to be the president, I know it is impossible. Rob and Paul are the two strongest contestants. I don't like both, but I would prefer Rob; Paul is just too idealistic. He lives in a fool's paradise."

Sensing an opening, Joshua asked about Rob and his views about the Board.

"Rob is a dictator. He loves power; he craves power. However, he is lenient on those who are in his good books; thank God I am one of them. Otherwise, Rob can be as ruthless as anyone."

"Sheriff, can I meet Rob with you?"

"Sure… but why?"

"Just for a small talk."

"OK."

Going back to his room, Joshua hatched a plan, a plan to turn the biggest adversary of the Board—the

Club—into its biggest pawn. And it involved Rob, with a little bit of Sheriff.

Rob was similar to the Sheriff's description, which made life easy for Joshua.

"Hello, Rob. How are you? I am Joshua; Sheriff's old friend."

"Fine. Yeah, he told me about you. You wanted to meet me. Any specific reasons?" Rob questioned Joshua to know exactly what the Board director was thinking when planning a meeting with the Club's to-be president.

"I like it, Rob. Straight to the point. Good. Well, we at the Board want to patch up with you. I know we have done something, but now we are mending our ways. You know, even IAAC and other bodies are recognizing our efforts. So why not join hands and work together? Anyways, if the world accounting bodies are not going to take you seriously, you will lose relevance. I don't think a leader like you would want that.

Come and join us. We will declare you as our subsidiary office in the United States. You get to remain president forever if you want to. And some additional financial support also," saying that Joshua winked at Sheriff.

Sheriff knew the meaning of that wink very well.

"We working together; not possible. What made you think that way?" Rob almost shouted and stood up to leave.

Before Joshua could say anything, Sheriff interrupted.

"Rob, I think we should consider Josh's proposal. Over the years, people have lost that vibe and are just meandering along. That anti-Board sentiment is long gone after the James' days. And we wanted the Board to work as per the principles and facilitate the junior members. If they are willing to do that, we should help them."

Joshua smiled quietly; his friend had taken his bait.

"So, Rob, what do you think? Give our proposal a thought. It is mutually beneficial. Yes, you have support among the masses, but all the official bodies recognize us as the accounting body of our country. Do you want to live as number two, Rob?" Joshua tried to incite Rob's ego, and it worked.

"Give me some time to think over it. But I want to ask one thing: how can you help me win the president's elections?"

"We have connections, Rob. Just trust us," Joshua said while taking a sip of coffee.

Just days before the voting, the Club witnessed an exuberant rise in its members. The spike clearly took everyone by surprise. Rob and Sheriff were talking about it in their office when Joshua called.

"Hey, Rob, how are you?"

"Fine. What's up at your side?"

"Hope you are observing the rise in the members? Well, you are welcome for the votes."

"Is that you, Joshua?" Rob couldn't help but ask.

"I told you, Rob, we have connections. Now enjoy your win and pay heed to my advice."

"Sure."

"Good. See you soon then, Rob," with that, Joshua disconnected the line and boarded the plane. He couldn't wait to inform the directors about his achievement. More importantly, it would help him beat Aron and become the Board's president.

"Aron, you are finished," Joshua said under his breath and switched off his mobile.

In a month's time, after winning the elections, Rob invited all of the Board's directors to Houston and announced his plans to work together for the benefit of their professional community. Aron, in return, announced to make the Club the representative company of the Board in the United States. He further added that an official communique would be released to inform all concerned. The merger allowed Rob full support from the mother organization, with Sheriff being his number two. Rob had already talked to the other directors of the Club regarding the new development; they all agreed except Paul. He resigned, questioning the intentions of his colleagues.

"Soon, the Club will be what the Board is—a group of corrupt demigods," saying that Paul, left the room, vowing never to return.

Chapter Two: The Challenger

Rob's ascend to the top of the Club saw drastic changes in the priorities of the organization. He and his team slowly cut down on the anti-Board narrative, citing the image of the country as the main reason. Moreover, they galvanized their efforts in finding better opportunities for their members. In a board meeting, Rob consented that allowing young professionals an opportunity to build their network in a foreign country should be the primary concern of the Club. He added that given the financial meltdown, it was their moral obligation as seniors to help junior members find better jobs, which would benefit the country in the form of remittances.

Though not all the members agreed with this approach, they also realized that the world was going through one of the worst economic crises. Therefore, a change of course was required, albeit temporarily.

Ensuring job placement for those who have lost their jobs was indeed the need of the hour, though it was not on the Club's original manifesto; issues with the Board could be resolved later on. The 2008 Recession proved to be a game-changer for Rob, providing him with enough space to assert his position. His novice presidency was given the cushion it needed to lay the solid foundations of a prolonged rule.

Successful dealing with the Club won Joshua the presidency of the Board for the next year. Apart from being a qualified accountant, he was an accomplished businessman. He was a partner of an audit firm and was also in the management of one of the leading accounting colleges in the country. Joshua surely knew how to make safe investments. And with the Club onboard, he has opened for himself another business opportunity. Taking advantage of the precarious financial situation, he colluded with Rob and Sheriff to start hiring professionals cheaply for their overseas company. The allure of working in the U.S. was too much for the young graduates to resist. As they boarded the planes for America, thinking about making it big in the country of their dreams, Joshua was overjoyed about the extra income stream. At the same time, Rob was happy to have minions at his disposal as junior members. Surely, they wouldn't dare to go against him and his policies.

The assumption of having enough numbers to subdue his opposition within the Club turned Rob into a dictator. With the additional power and continued financial support from Joshua, he started to showcase his true colors.

Rob originally belonged to the lower-middle class. He was an intelligent student and had a never-say-die personality. Despite the financial challenges, he managed to enroll himself in an accounting college. Knowing his father wouldn't be able to afford his tuition fees, Rob worked part-time while studying. His hard work soon paid off as he was offered a job as a junior auditor in one of the leading firms. He was excited to be a part of a multinational company, but little did he know that his life would change for the worse. The emotional and mental abuse he endured during that period mutilated his personality no end. Soon, his dynamic nature was turned upside down with only a one-point agenda for life: attain great power to make others bow down to him. He was willing to do anything to achieve his goals; coercion or bribe, anything would do for him. As long as he was getting the desired results, he didn't care about the means; for Rob, the end justified the means. Even relationships were based on benefits. His whole life was a profit and loss statement.

Rob's ability to get all the problems sorted made him famous in the financial sector. He was viewed as the problem-solver, a man with the right connections, by the top management and was greatly in demand. While working for one of the clients, he got the opportunity to work for an American company. The owners were planning to acquire a company in

Houston and were looking for a reliable accountant. They shared their view with Rob, who immediately accepted the offer. Working in the U.S. was perfect for him, a country where hard work is acknowledged and provides excellent networking opportunities. Climbing up the organizational ladder was easier and less time-consuming, which is precisely what Rob wanted.

When Rob landed in America, the country was experiencing an economic boom. Properties, residential or commercial, were selling like hotcakes, which propelled the financial sector as well. It allowed ample opportunities for him to showcase his expertise. Shortly, he was able to win the confidence of his management and was promoted to the managerial position. With position came power and possibilities of meeting with other successful professionals. That's when he met Paul and Henry, who informed him about the Club and its objectives. Being one of the victims of the system, Rob decided to enroll in the Club. While his inner conscience wanted him to work for the betterment of his fellow accountants, his lust for power was too great to be suppressed. Not someone to shy away from hard work, Rob worked diligently to create awareness about the Club and was rewarded with the position of team leader when the first core committee was sworn in.

Not satisfied with the middle-level position, Rob wanted to be at the top; he wanted to be president. However, there were other strong candidates as well. While working in the US, Rob learned one thing: one can't have his cake and eat it too. He has to share some of the spoils with others along the way in order to get to the top; you take some, you give some. Otherwise, he would forever remain alone, without any support from colleagues or subordinates. The shift in his mindset allowed him to rationally analyze the potential resources at his disposal. He recognized Paul as the potential threat because of his loyalty to the cause. However, others could be used for personal goals, especially Sheriff and Ellis. According to his assessment, they both were self-driven and were more likely to change sides. Moreover, if given their quota, they were not the ones to threaten his supremacy. Thus, he aligned with Sheriff and Ellis and assured them of mutual benefits for siding with him. Just as the three were planning to mount a strong challenge against Paul, Joshua met them with his plan. The timing couldn't have been better for Rob.

Paul, on the other hand, was an ideologue and had immense popularity among the founding members of the Club. To beat him to the presidency wouldn't be easy. That's where additional memberships provided by Joshua made such a huge difference in Rob's favor. However, he was not doing it out of sympathy. For his favors, Joshua, too, required some support; you give some, you take some. Rob was well-versed in that. Coming together of two (evil) masterminds proved enormous. Their different personality styles complemented each other perfectly. While Rob was authoritative, Joshua was diplomatic, and together they formed a killer combination.

Throughout the Great Recession, Joshua and Rob Nexus made millions. Though on paper, they were providing junior accountants with a working opportunity in the U.S., they were paying those poor souls peanuts compared to what they were making. Additionally, the move provided Rob with enough junior members to keep him at the top of the Club.

Things were going smoothly until one of their exports to the U.S. raised a dissenting voice; her name was Olive. A young lady in her mid-thirties, Olive was ambitious, brave, strong-willed, and confident. Like Rob, she also belonged to the middle class of her country. Her primary objective in joining the Club was to raise her voice against the adverse conditions in which juniors were forced to work and to allow more meaningful women participation. Coming from a country with strong patriarchal roots, Olive was a curious case, almost too good to be true.

Unlike other women, Olive's priorities were different. She firmly believed in the equality of genders and raised her voice at every available forum for the cause. However, she was not someone who only wanted rights; she was equally mindful of her responsibilities. In her view, society couldn't function properly without mutual and equal contributions from both men and women. She believed in it and was prepared to go the extra mile. Her hard-working nature even convinced some of the anti-feminists in the Club. Earlier, there was a general belief that women work less but demand more, but not Olive. She used to put in the same amount of effort as any of her male counterparts to get the job done. And it was not for showboating. Olive never indulged in such practices. Her modus operandi was simple: work hard and honestly so that it becomes your recognition among your peers and social circles.

Being a successful working woman didn't mean Olive was ignorant of her domestic responsibilities. On the contrary, she was a loving wife and a caring mother. Home was her only recluse from all the work-related worries and exertion. Mathew and Olive got married five years ago and have two sons. They both managed their professional lives in such a way as to give maximum time to their families, especially their kids. For Mathew, COVID-19 has simplified matters a lot. Being an I.T. guy, he was allowed to work from home and was only required to come to the office in cases of emergency or meetings. His flexible work settings also allowed Olive to concentrate more on her social activities, something she always cherished but couldn't perform due to family. Hence, she decided to take part as an active member of the Club. That's when the boat started to rock.

The Rob-Joshua juggernaut that has been going on so smoothly for years was identified and blamed for all the wrongdoing they have committed under the guise of maintaining a professional networking platform. It disturbed the whole bureaucracy of the organization.

Till now, whoever has tried to point the finger against Rob for all his malpractices was either bribed or sidelined. He had his own peculiar style of quashing his opposition. Thus, when Olive started to object to the inconsistencies of the Club's top management, everyone tried to silence her. Some, out of their genuine concern for her, wanted her to cut down on her scathing criticism because they knew Rob. They advised Olive to be less vocal or leave the Club; there was no third option. However, she was not someone who would bow down easily to an oppressor, especially if he controlled the lives and futures of hundreds and thousands of qualified people.

***

"Hi, Olive."

"Hello, Grace. What's up? You look drowsy? Girl, what were you doing last night?" Olive smiled mischievously at her friend.

"It is not what you are thinking. Yesterday, I was at the Club, sorting out things for the upcoming meeting.

Got home late," Grace replied yawningly. "I need a coffee badly; wait."

When Grace returned with her coffee from the pantry, Olive was busy with her work.

"Come on, Olive, what are you working on? We have already emailed the reports; chill."

"I was checking some data as a heads-up for the next month," Olive replied.

"We have time for that, miss extra efficient. Close it, please."

"It won't take much…."

"Are you doing it, or should I?"

Not wanting to disappoint her best friend in the new country, Olive pressed the cross button on the top-right corner of the window and locked her computer.

"OK, sleeping beauty, go ahead."

"You bring something for lunch today?" Grace asked.

"Yes."

"Good. Bring it out; let's have breakfast."

"Hello…."

"Olive, I am desperately hungry. I will get you pizza delivered for lunch."

"Large pepperoni with extra cheese."

"What?"

"Your call. If you want my sandwiches, you have to deliver me the pizza of my choice," demanded Olive.

"OK, let's go to the dining area," Grace surrendered, knowing she didn't have a better alternative. Ordering something from an outlet would take at least twenty minutes, and she was not in the mood to wait.

"And what is desperately hungry?"

"Now, don't start correcting my English."

They both stared at each other for a moment and then started laughing.

"How was your weekend? Mmm…this is so tasty. Yummilicious. Did you make it yourself? What's the sauce?" Grace asked a volley of questions in a go.

"Thanks, on behalf of Mat; he made it. Weekend was awesome; we went sightseeing. You tell?"

"Lucky you. I was stuck with the Club's work. Monthly general meeting is coming up, and I have volunteered to be the announcer," Grace replied, taking a bite of the sandwich.

"What is the name of your club?" Olive asked.

"Club; that's the name."

"So, what does your Club do?"

"The Club is the overseas arm of the Board and works for the promotion of accounts and financial professionals in the U.S. You can say it provides a networking platform for certified accountants from our country, like us, in this country. We do promotional activities where top corporate executives are invited and help get qualified accountants jobs here. Similarly, there are some fund-raising activities for social causes. We also engage with the consulate staff to commemorate national days. Remember, Alan and I were discussing about a meeting a week back; it was the same."

"That's great. I like it. Can I become a member as well?"

"Yeah, sure. Accompany me this Friday evening. Haven't you heard of the Club before?"

"Can't recall if I did."

"Surprised. When did you come to Houston?"

"2016."

"And it is 2018, two years, and you don't know about the Club despite being my friend?" Grace couldn't hide her astonishment.

"Well, you didn't introduce it this way before," replied Olive, seemingly unconcerned of Grace's bewilderment.

Olive was fascinated with the idea of mingling with her compatriots in a professional setting. It had been a couple of years since she came to the U.S. to be with her husband. Though she liked her adopted country, its professionalism, opportunities, freedom, and equality, she missed her home. According to Mathew, it was normal for Olive to feel nostalgic about their country. But now she has the opportunity to meet her people. *Maybe I could meet some of my batchmates,* she thought.

The week passed in a wink, and it was time for Olive to accompany Grace to her Club. She was excited. After the day's work, they both went to the Club's office; meeting preparations were underway. Grace introduced Olive to her team leader, Robert and Ellis.

"He is one of the directors and heads the event management team," Grace whispered into Olive about Ellis.

Grace left Olive to rehearse for the announcements. Finding Ellis comparatively free, she went to him to get more information about the organization and the membership process. He was very accommodating and encouraged Olive to attend the general meeting on coming Sunday.

"We want young and energetic professionals like you to carry forward our mission," he said. "I will look forward to meeting you, and don't worry about the membership; consider it done."

April 2019: almost a year after Olive joined the Club. Upon reaching the thousand-member figure, the management threw a party for all the affiliates. She was enjoying her meal with the team in the canteen of the organization when she heard a gray-haired man grumbling about something. He was sitting with a group of middle-aged people and didn't look happy. His agitated gestures caught everyone's attention.

"Fools. Do they think by throwing a teenage party like this, they can hide their corruption? Are we dumb?"

"He is Harry, right?" Olive asked Alan.

"Yeah, crazy, Harry. He is always mad over something."

"But what corruption is he talking about?"

"Don't know; neither am I interested?"

"At least check."

"Ms 'Socialworker' Olive, we are here to enjoy the party, not to listen to a lecture," Grace retorted.

Oblivious of her friends' disapproval, Olive went to Harry and listened intently.

"Rob thinks that with Joshua at his back, he can do anything. He is mistaken."

"What do you mean by that, Harry? What has Rob done wrong?" asked Olive.

"Girl, you are new to this place; you don't know. This Rob-Joshua duo is up to no good. They are enticing young accountants to come to America and work for them. Both are making money but are paying them chicken feed with zero facilities. These poor guys are nothing but fodder for their greed."

"Are you sure? Do you have proof?"

"Proof? Are you asking me for proof? Ask Rob why he is not conducting the audit for the last year's expenses. Where are the financials of 2017?"

Olive asked the same questions from Robert, her team leader, but he didn't have an answer. When we got up to check with Ellis, Robert stopped her.

"Olive, leave it; enjoy the party. What's the point in raising these issues?"

"Two reasons: first, they are playing with the futures of young professionals, and second, accountability. As qualified accountants, aren't we supposed to be the torchbearers of accountability and compliance?"

Robert didn't reply, which made Olive to go to Ellis' office; however, he was not present. Coming back, she went to Harry and asked him about the details.

"I will put the matter to the governing board. Will you help me?" she asked Harry.

"Will see, girl," was all he replied.

***

Olive's persistence over the years encouraged Harry, Alan, and Grace to join her. Though Harry was one of the founding members, he was sidelined by the pro-Rob group, due to which he became delusional but didn't leave the Club like Paul. He was an ideologue who believed in James' philosophy against the corrupt Board. Thus, when Olive started raising her voice, he was the first person to join her. His alliance with Olive also persuaded some old loyalists to support her.

Unlike Harry, Alan and Grace were Olive's contemporaries. They were hard-working professionals who couldn't stay silent and ignored all the irregularities at the Club. Coming from the same system and enduring the same amount of hardship as Olive, they came out in the open and demanded more transparency in the Club's financial matters. Since Olive, Alan, and Grace were of the same age and used to hang out together, people used to call them like-minded. When they started to oppose Rob's dictatorship, the term became their identity. Soon, every dissenting voice was labeled as Like-Minded by their opponents. In return, Olive and her mates started calling Rob and the current ruling elite Unionists in reference to the Irish political workers who supported unification with Great Britain. They contended that Rob and his accomplices had unified the Club with the Board and were making money for themselves without regard for junior members.

Chapter Three: The (Inconceivable) Fall

Soon, the idea, which started in the Club's canteen, gained ground among the members. Rob's high-handedness was making everyone apprehensive. They wanted the organization to come clean and respond to the accusations by openly disclosing the records of their yearly expenditures. The overriding sentiment was that the directors were taking kickbacks from vendors while awarding contracts for events. The fact that the management has not officially declared the financials for the last three years further added fuel to the suspicions. Moreover, a human resource services provider was recently hired for the placement of the members. Interestingly, though, the company's top brass was Rob's acquaintances.

Initially, the directors cited the lockdown as an excuse, promising to work on preparing the statements once the matters settled. However, the promise was not honored, and even after a gap of three years, there were no signs of revealing the information to the public. Sensing the management's seeming lack of interest in walking the talk, people raised the point during general members' meetings. According to the constitution of the Club, the board of directors has to hold at least one meeting with all its affiliates in a month, appraising them about their initiatives and plans for the future.

Fearing the severity of the backlash to intensify, which could lead to an unsavory situation, the administration decided to cut down on the number of general meetings, with Rob and other directors missing the majority of them to avoid cross-questioning. Also, based on the Sheriff's idea, the working committee decided to hold general meetings on weekdays instead of weekends and holidays. When objection was raised, the committee replied with the shortage of funds and the non-availability of spaces to hold such large gatherings. Rob and his team of directors knew they couldn't hold back on the meetings for too long, or they would have to face a legal battle. Therefore, they tried to the fullest to create hurdles to reduce attendance naturally. However, it didn't mean they were not doing anything illegal. They were just trying to wrap them up legally.

Furthermore, team leaders and other office bearers were instructed to give the names of the conforming members so that, moving forward, the presence of pro-Rob members could be ensured in all the meetings to counter the Like-Minded narrative. Publication of the official newsletter was also put temporarily on hold to control the flow of information. The idea was to isolate the dissenting voices with the assumption that soon others would forget about them. Little did the Club's management know that such marginalization tactics were only working against the president and his accomplices. Those who at first were not serious about the charges and took them as scams started to take notice of the development. The arrogance with which Rob was handling the matter was not winning him any friends. On the contrary, he was only affording his critics more credibility and prominence.

Noticing the simmering condition, Sheriff decided to talk with Rob. He wanted Rob to show some flexibility and calm down the matter. Sheriff feared that the prevailing scenario would not be beneficial for the incumbent. It was not as if Sheriff had a soft corner for Rob; he was only thinking about his directorship. Due to his unconditional support for Rob over the years, people in the Club view Sheriff as his main man. Thus, he would also suffer the consequences in case anti-Rob sentiment managed to achieve success.

"So, Sheriff, tell me, what you wanted to talk about?"

"Rob, I think you are going overboard. We can't just keep Like-Minded away like this. In my opinion, it is better to talk with them and find out a solution."

"Oh, come on. Don't tell me…, are you scared of them?" Rob taunted. "What do you think a bunch of novices can do to me?"

"It is not about being scared. Don't forget they are members of this Club; they have paid the fees. Legally, we can't hide information from them because it is mentioned in the constitution of our organization. If they come to know about it, they can sue us. This is the U.S., and they have rights." Sheriff emphasized the latter part to instill some sense into Rob.

"And who will tell them? You…, me…?"

"Be practical, Rob; in this age of social media, do you think we can prevent them? Don't forget, our office bearers used to work with them; they were colleagues, some were friends. We can't prevent any information leakage. And if that happens, it will spell doom for us; you know that. Can you keep all those working at the Club tight-lipped forever? No. No one can guarantee that. So, why take such a big risk?"

"Sheriff, clearly you are shaken by their demands. You are free to switch sides, but I will not lie down easily. Come to think of it, after all, I… we did for them; they have the nerve to stand against us!" Rob was clearly furious.

"You are being childish now, Rob. We have also made money, so it's even-stevens. Secondly, we didn't pay out of our pockets; we just used the money we received from their fee. And what about the 'promotional grant' we get from the Board? What if they come to know that the amount is to promote our professionals in the U.S. through P.R. events? You know better than me how much we are actually spending for the purpose, not even one-third. Rob, clearly, you are being disillusioned and taking matters far too personally. Snap out before it's too late," saying that Sheriff left the room. He had realized it was useless to talk with him in this mood. He had always known Rob as authoritative and not the one to take criticism easily, but he would descend to such a low level was hard to comprehend. *How can he not see the writing on the wall*, Sheriff thought.

The Club's original sources of revenue were the annual membership fee and sales from their monthly newsletter. However, since Joshua assumed the presidency of the Board, he got a monthly grant of $10,000 approved by the Supreme Council. On paper, the allowance was for promoting the organization and young professionals in the U.S. market and creating a network within the country. In reality, it was anything but otherwise. Considering they were from a developing country, the issuance of the grant on a monthly basis did raise some alarms, both at the Club and the Board, but with Joshua at the helm, Rob and his board members didn't have to worry about anything. Like other matters at the Board, the Club was not accountable for the amount and was never made to show any records to prove the expenditure.

***

"Nice pic, girl," Grace commented on Regina's Instagram status with a thumbs-up emoji.

"Thanks," Regina immediately replied with a heart.

"What's the occasion?"

"It was a meeting at the Club," Regina replied nonchalantly. "Why weren't you guys present?" she went on to ask Grace.

Completely shocked to know of a meeting taking place at the Club without them being informed, Grace immediately called Regina.

"Hey. Where are you right now?"

"Just leaving the Convention Center."

"Was Olive there?" Grace asked.

"No, none of your gang was there," replied Regina. "OK, Grace, listen. I got to hang up; I am getting in the car; can't talk while driving."

"Sure. Take care, bye."

Grace disconnected the call, unsure what to make of what she had just heard. *A Club meeting… without any invitation to us!* She still couldn't digest it.

"Hey, Olive, what's up," Grace said.

"Nothing, girl, just making dinner," Olive replied.

"You at home? Didn't you attend the meeting?" Grace asked, trying to decipher whether Olive knew about it or not.

"Which meeting?" Olive asked in return.

Realizing the Club hadn't informed them about the meeting, Grace informed Olive about the event and sent Regina's photo to prove her point. Equally shaken as Grace, Olive asked her to stay put while she checked with other Like-Minded people. After making more than a dozen calls, Olive got the hang of things and decided to share it with everyone. She put all the gang members on a group call and discussed the new happenings with them.

Needless to say, they all were stunned; however, they decided to lay low and find out whether this was the first instance or had been happening for long. Harry, the eldest of them all, advised them not to react abruptly. Rather, they plan their actions wisely as Rob and his cohorts had presented them with a huge opportunity. He instructed them to wait for the next three to four months and gather evidence that showed that the Club had been organizing events without informing them. Then, they could pressure the board of directors to make way or face a legal battle. As members of the Club, they couldn't be kept in the dark about any event taking place in the organization. Acknowledging the significance of the matter, everyone agreed with Harry and decided to wait for their moment.

They didn't have to wait for long. After a couple of months, the Club held another meeting without informing Olive and her confederates. Again, Regina was the source of information. After ensuring that none of the Like-Minded members received the invitation, Olive wrote a scathing email to the board of directors, demanding an explanation. She told them how she and her friends came to know about meetings and other social gatherings taking place at the Club's platform without them getting any invitation. She was happy to have cornered Rob and others and thought about forcing them to quit and hold fresh elections. While thinking about the prospect, Olive's thoughts were disturbed by the tune of a new notification informing her that she had received an email. Hurriedly, she opened it and came in for the biggest shock of her life.

Dear Ms. Olive,

This is with reference to your earlier email that the Club is entitled to inform and invite all its members to any meeting and public gathering of note. Please be informed that according to a board of directors' decision dated March 13, 2021, the Club is only entitled to inform and invite all its A and Premium Class members to every meeting; invitations to the B and C Class members would be conditional, subject to the availability of space.

Since you and the names you mentioned in your email are B Class members, you can't hold the Club accountable for not inviting you.

Hope to have clarified the matter.

Thanks and regards,

Angelina,

Secretary,

The Club

P.S. Attached is a copy of the decision. It has been approved by the Board.

Olive just stared at the monitor, not knowing what to do. Not even in her dreams she had thought of such a thing. Reluctantly, she opened the attachment and went through the document. It sure said what the email had mentioned. The board's approval seal was also present. She thought about asking why, as a member, she was not notified about the decision but quickly rejected the idea. After the Board's approval, the Club's management was not liable to explain the matter, and neither Rob nor his team would provide any. *What to do now? Have we been booted out of the Club?* With those thoughts in her mind, Olive leaned back on the reclining chair and closed her eyes. Her Sunday has just changed for the worse.

***

Soon after meeting with Rob, Sheriff realized he had to think of something quickly on his own; otherwise, they would be left with nothing. He knew Like-Minded's demands were genuine and couldn't be held off for long. Therefore, they have to find a way to find a legal cover. It will not take Olive and her team long to discover what Sheriff and his colleagues had been doing. *Olive is a smart young lady backed by that sly old ideologue, Harry. We need to be careful while dealing with them,* Sheriff thought. However, judging from Rob's tone, it was evident he was not grasping the gravity of the situation. *Unwarranted stubbornness would cost us everything; this was the time for keeping a calmer head.*

"Think, Sheriff, think," he muttered under his breath, sipping his glass.

The next day, Sheriff went early to the Club's office. He had scheduled a meeting with Jacob, a legal attorney. They had been friends for almost a decade. Sheriff was hoping for sound advice from his trusted friend. Before leaving, he called Angelina, the secretary, to take out the Club's constitution and other legal documents. He didn't want to waste a minute in finding the required file.

Jacob arrived on time and, from Sheriff's expressions, could make it that it was serious stuff. Jacob hadn't seen him so anxiously worried before.

"Speak up, man; what's bothering you?" Jacob finally asked.

"Jacob, my buddy. These are the legal files of the Club; you can read them later at your office. I will ask the maintenance staff to put them in your car. First, listen very carefully to what I have to say."

Sheriff narrated the whole scenario to Jacob and looked expectedly at him.

"Interesting. Let me go through the documents; only then can I say anything," Jacob said carelessly, trying to defuse the tension, and asked, "Where are we going for lunch?"

Sheriff knew his lawyer friend's choice well and took him to Navy Blue.

After a week, Jacob called Sheriff and delivered the good news.

"You said that you have the backing of at least fifty percent of your members, right?"

"Yes," Sheriff replied hastily.

"OK, now, listen carefully. Divide your members into different categories, like A, B, and C. Pass a ruling that the Club will be liable only to notify so and so class members of all the activities, get the voting done on the ruling, send it to your principal organization, and get it approved. This way, no one can touch you."

"But is it possible to make that classification?" Sheriff asked.

"Yeah, the Club's constitution affords veto powers to the president. He can make decisions of high importance without the consent of the directors. Conversely, he can also veto the decisions of the directors."

"Wow, good. Didn't know that veto powers would one day come in handy. But how do we classify the members? Based on what criterion?"

"What is your organizational hierarchy?" asked the lawyer.

"President, then directors, then regional heads looking after different regions of the country, then area heads, and then team leaders."

"I hope none of your opponents hold any powerful office in the Club?"

"No."

"Perfect. Make the classification based on the responsibilities of each individual. For example, assign a premium category to regional heads, an A category to area heads, a B category to team leaders, and a C category to regular members. Hold on, I think I got the wording for you. The Club will be liable only to notify Premium and A class members of all the activities. Invitations to B and C class members will be subject to the availability of space. How's that?" Jacob asked Sheriff triumphantly.

"I know you can find something for us. Thanks, old buddy. Tonight's dinner and drinks are on the house; just let me know the time and location. See you then."

Sheriff called on all the board directors and appraised them of the situation. They all were overjoyed except Rob. Though he thanked Sheriff for his efforts, deep inside, he felt suspicious. *Is Sheriff trying to take over me,* he thought.

In no time, the directors put to work Jacob's instructions and got the document approved by the Board. Legally, they were safe from the Liked-Minded and free to continue their merry way. It called for a celebration.

"Angelina, send an email to all the members, no, only our allies, to join us in our celebration on March 20, 2021, at the Convention Center," Rob shouted the instructions to his secretary and left the room.

When Rob reached the Convention Center, he saw people praising and congratulating Sheriff. They were not just normal members; they were the crux of the Club. A sense of jealousy and insecurity awash him. Rob liked Sheriff for his support throughout the years and, more importantly, for linking him up with Joshua. At that moment, though, he was envious of his main man for taking all the limelight.

Watching Rob entering, Sheriff reached out to him with drinks in his hands.

"Hey, Mr. President, let's toast together."

"Sure."

They all partied hard that day and were extremely happy, except for one man, Rob. The way other directors were lavishing praise on Sheriff made him mad. Eventually, he lost his sanity to envy and busted out at him in front of everyone. Realizing that Rob was drunk, Sheriff tried to cover up the matter, but Rob was having none of it. He accused Sheriff of plotting against him to get the top post.

"Rob, you are not in your senses. Stop embarrassing yourself and leave," shouted Sheriff.

"Now, you will instruct me. I am the boss here, and you are just my subordinate. Remember the difference; you better remember it."

Sheriff left the center immediately feeling low. He was sad that Rob misbehaved but also happy that he got to know of Rob's real intentions.

"Mr. President, if I can save your ass, I can knock it off also," he said, driving his car out of the parking lot.

The next day, Sheriff called Joshua.

"Hey, Josh. How are you?"

"Fine. What's up? What made you call me?"

"Can't I call for a chat?" Sheriff said, mocking anger.

"Sheriff, my man, I have known you for twenty years. Cut the chase; I am all ears."

Sheriff then cooked up a story, telling Joshua how Rob was planning to overthrow him.

"Josh, Rob has money; he is in the U.S., and he knows all your directors. It will not take him long to get them to his side."

"But will he come here," Joshua was confused but couldn't overlook Sheriff's warning.

"It will take only half a day to reach there. Rob can be here and manage the Board as well. For him, it will not be a big problem. You know he is a traveling freak."

***

After deliberating upon the matter for some time, Olive decided to inform others. She put everyone on the group call and shared what she had learned.

"I knew these old guards would do anything to stay in power," howled Harry.

"Now, what will we do?" Alan voiced his concern. "Is there any way out for us?"

"As far as I know, no. However, I think rather than surrendering, why not shoot an email to the Board directed to Joshua? Inform him that all this was done without any prior notice," advised Harry.

"But Joshua and Rob are one the same," said Olive hopelessly. "Do you think he will consider our email?"

"Never die wondering, young lady. We don't have any other choice. And if we delay, then the Board will time-barred our concern," the old Harry said.

Taking a cue from Harry, Olive wrote an email to the President of the Board, Joshua, explaining to him all that had happened and how, as the members of the

Club, they felt left out. Upon receiving the email, Joshua contacted Sheriff and shared with him the latest development.

"Josh, this is the time to make your move against Rob; pre-empt him."

"What do you mean?" Joshua asked.

"Forward this email to Rob and ask him sternly to explain the matter; otherwise, you will dissolve the board and announce fresh voting for the Club. Knowing Rob and his big ego, he will find it hard to come to terms with your order. Then you can dissolve the board," explained Sheriff.

"Let me see," Joshua said and hung up.

The next morning, he called Rob.

"Rob, I have received an email from Ms. Olive. She has blamed you for keeping the members in the dark. I have talked with Sheriff …"

Hearing Sheriff's name, Rob busted out on Joshua.

"So you two have combined against me. I always knew Sheriff was a backstabber, but you! Listen to me, Josh; we were in it together. If anything happens to me?" Rob said threateningly.

"So you are threatening me?" Joshua asked. He was clearly surprised, but then he recalled what Sheriff had told, and everything seemed to fall in place for him.

"Rob, I, as the President of the Board, order you to refute the claim made against you, or I will dissolve the Club's governing board," Joshua commanded. "You will receive an official email shortly."

"No need for the email, Josh. Don't tire your fingers; I am resigning," Rob shouted and immediately disconnected the call.

"So, Sheriff was right," Joshua murmured and went out of his room to instruct his secretary to send an official email to the Club.

Chapter Four: Change of Guards

The call from Joshua shook Rob badly. He couldn't believe Sheriff and Joshua would ditch him at this critical juncture. The two persons he trusted the most. Over the years, they have developed a strong bond, and considering their intertwined interests, Rob was not expecting a rude and sudden shut-up call from them. What alarmed Rob even more was that they knew all his secrets. While others respected him, either genuinely or out of fear, and held him in high regard, in front of Sheriff and Joshua, the king was naked.

Rob spent the night pacing his room to find a way out of the quagmire. First, he lost Sheriff, and now Joshua. *This couldn't be good and needs to be stopped. But how?* Being more of an enforcer than a thinker, Rob, for once, was finding himself out of his depth. Appeasing people to get them along was not his forte. He had learned to share the spoils with others, provided they were ready to accept him as in charge; bending over to give explanations for his actions was never in his books. Throughout his time at the helm, Sheriff used to come up with ideas to pre-empt any opposition, only for Rob to enforce them. With Rob, it was my way or the highway. After assuming the Club's presidency, the dictator in him had fully taken over his personality, which meant zero tolerance for differences in opinion and no chance of taking a backstep. Remorse and turnaround were words unknown to him.

Also, Rob was an out-and-out traditionalist in his approach and thought process, with little room for flexibility. He liked following a pre-defined template rather than exploring different situations to learn or find something new and exciting. Hence, changes have always been a nuisance for him since they require altering one's style and coming up with out-of-box ideas. Accepting a change as a last resort when no other option was possible has been Rob's mantra. And it was more to ward off the danger or minimize the damage.

In Like-Minded and Olive, though, he has to confront the biggest change and challenge of his professional life. Change because a group of young and energetic accountants was raising their voices, demanding answers from the seniors about their past doings. It was not something the veterans like Rob could fathom easily or appreciate. However, the problem was that their concerns were genuine and not unjustified. Another factor, though Rob was unwilling to recognize, was the fact that a young lady was challenging him. He couldn't come to terms with the notion of ceding the Club's reigns to a woman, no matter how dynamic and talented she was. To him, men have the sole right to lead an organization.

Notwithstanding his antipathy towards being answerable to someone, especially juniors and women, Rob couldn't hush away the matter. He had to respond to their questions; there were no two ways about that.

Otherwise, it would mark the end of his supremacy. Worst still, he has to do that without his strongest ally, Sheriff, by his side.

***

The email from Joshua sent ripples across the Club. All the Unionists were surprised by the turn of events. Not long ago, they celebrated a (supposed) victory against Like-Minded after getting the Board's approval for the directors' ruling. Now, out of nowhere, came an email from the president. It was more of a show-cause notice for Rob and his team to come good against Olive and Like-Minded's allegations.

"Sheriff, what is the meaning of this email?" Ellis, one of the directors, asked.

"Ask your president, not me. Didn't you hear him at the Convention Center? I am just his subordinate."

"We know what Rob did was wrong; he shouldn't have burst out in front of all the people, considering the occasion and everything. But this is serious stuff. For once, come out of your personal bubble and think about us all. The Board is asking for the missing financial statements and has given us only three months for that. You know we haven't prepared our financials for the last three years; how will that be possible in the given time?" Ellis' voice was bordering on rage and uncertainty. It seemed he was dumbfounded and was not sure how to react. Well, he was not alone; everyone was, except Sheriff.

He continued, "Joshua, the Board president, is your friend, right? Talk to him and ask for a way out."

"I am not asking anyone for any favors anymore, Ellis. Not for that man, at least," Sheriff said.

His commanding tone was enough to suggest to Ellis that Sheriff was in no mood to patch up with Rob. Therefore, Ellis hung up, fearing his and the board's immediate future. Not knowing what to do, he dialed Rob's number but to no avail.

After talking to Ellis, Sheriff called Joshua.

"It seems tremors shocks were felt in Houston," Sheriff quipped.

"Hahaha… Well, Rob asked for it. After talking with you, I called him. I wanted to know his side of the story, but he didn't let me finish and just blasted out. I think you were right; he had something to hide, and that's why he reacted that way," Joshua replied. "Anyways, tell me about yourself; what are you planning to do? If Rob fails the audit, you know it will not be good for you also. I will be left with no option but to announce new elections, and what I have learned from you or others, Like-Minded, will give you guys a tough challenge, to say the least."

"Hmm… let's see. First, I will observe what Rob is thinking and will plan accordingly. I don't mind rejoining him, given that he approaches me by himself. It seems someone is in need of a reality check. People living in their bubbles think they move the world; they are very important, and everyone thinks about them. Hello…, you are nobody. The world doesn't stop spinning for anyone, no matter how important you think you are. You'd better stop living in your self-created, delusional world and face the reality on the ground. If Rob thinks he is someone and can manage this situation, good luck. If he needs me, he should come to me. No point being Mr. Nice Guy anymore," Sheriff let go of all his emotions.

"Wow… wow… calm down. I know you are mad at Rob, but why me? I haven't done anything. Relax, I am still on your side," Joshua tried to cool his friend down. He knew there must be a strong reason behind Sheriff's outburst. Not a person to openly express his emotions, Sheriff has always been known as the cool-headed guy who would wait for his turn rather than going about things carelessly. Maybe that's why he liked chess: be patient and let your opponent make a mistake. True to his nature, Sheriff was again prepared to play the waiting game.

"Any chance to catch up in Toronto in a week's time? I will be there for ten days; some business stuff. I will let you know the exact days," Joshua said, trying to divert his friend's attention.

"Josh, you are a godsend. Some days away from this mess will not be a bad idea. Just let me know the dates, and I will be there."

"OK then, see you in Toronto," with that, Joshua disconnected the line.

The call calmed Sheriff's nerves a bit. After venting out his anger, he felt nice and easy. He was ready to plot some more mischief.

***

After Joshua's email, Rob decided to take some time off. Therefore, he took a leave from the Club and kept his mobile silent. He didn't want to interact with any of the Club's directors, team leaders, or secretaries. Consequently, he decided to visit Miami and enjoy the city's warm weather and pleasant beaches. For Rob, the freshness of the sea breeze has been the best reliever. It recharged his energies and freshened up his mood like nothing else. Whenever feeling down, he would go to a beach and immerse himself in the tranquility of the setting. This time also, it was no different.

One morning, relaxing under his ninja tent, Ron stumbled upon the idea of first finding out the source that leaked the information that a Club meeting was taking place. *I would not be surprised to find Sheriff behind all this. He had warned me about that; maybe he did it on purpose to prove his point,* thought Rob. He was still not prepared to acknowledge the fact that it was his mismanagement that prompted Like-Minded to start questioning the manner in which the Club was managed. But then again, that was Rob. In his world, he was the best, who could do no wrong. Likewise, this conundrum was of someone else's making.

Sheriff or one of his cohorts, perhaps, he thought while sipping his fresh orange juice. He decided to retract his decision to resign. He wanted to fight and show Sheriff that he could do it without him as well. "I still have three months; let's see what comes up. Even if I go down, I will not give an open field to Sheriff," he murmured.

"Hello, Ellis, how are you? Sorry, I missed your calls; was traveling. Are you free to talk?" Rob sent a voice message to his director, hoping to find the culprit. Being the one responsible for holding the Club's events, Ellis was in constant contact with the majority of junior members. Therefore, Rob thought of talking to him first, in case he had anything to share. He didn't have to wait much, as Ellis immediately called.

"Hey, Rob. How are you? Where are you?" Ellis was full of questions.

"I am fine and in Miami; what about you?" Rob tried to keep his reply as to the point as possible, not to get distracted from the purpose of the call.

"Good, good; enjoy. I'm afraid I can't say the same about myself. That email from the Board has got me worried; I don't know what to do. Sheriff is least interested; I don't know why. Plus, you were unapproachable. How are we going to fix this mess?"

"Listen, Ellis, first relax. I have a hunch Sheriff is behind this. He wanted to bring me down to get the presidency; your assertion has only strengthened the belief. However, I want proof to take action against him."

"So what are you going to do?"

"Ellis, I want you to check with the team leaders and other members to find the person who informed Like-Minded about the Club meeting."

"OK. Then?" Ellis couldn't comprehend what Rob was trying to do.

"Just do this first, and then I will let you know about the rest," Rob instructed and immediately disconnected to avoid Ellis' volley of questions.

Upon his return to Houston, the first person Rob talked to was Ellis. He had managed to track the person; it was Regina.

"Ellis, call her to the office. I want to talk to her to find the real motive. In the meantime, ask her team leader and associates to check whether she is in contact with Sheriff or not. I want full information; you got me?" Rob spelled out his instructions in no uncertain terms.

Rob was at his brutal best when Regina came over for a meeting. He accused her of leaking the Club's information and threatened her with the consequences. However, he couldn't get the desired information from her, whether Sheriff was involved or not. Similarly, Ellis' fact-finding team couldn't come up with anything substantial. Reluctantly, Rob has to let Regina go. She was completely distraught coming out of the room and was visibly shivering. The Club's staff, after noticing her condition, tried to calm her down. She was, though, having none of it. Immediately, she called Grace and updated her on all that had happened to her.

"You, girl, calm down, don't panic," Grace tried to comfort her friend.

"Grace, you don't know how badly they treated me," Regina replied, sobbing.

"You know what, let's meet at the Golden Arches. I will contact Olive and see if she can make it, too. In the meantime, you relax, don't drive if you are not feeling well, just walk the distance," the protective Grace showed through.

"Just come quickly; I am waiting," Regina was finding it hard to control her emotions.

Within the next 15 minutes, Grace and Olive were in the restaurant, trying to reason why they behaved like that with Regina.

"I know Rob is an authoritative guy, but this behavior is unheard of," Olive was clearly confused. "What were they asking you?" he turned toward Regina and asked.

"They somehow got to know that I was the one who informed you guys about the meeting and was incensed at me. But instead of questioning me about you, Olive, they were more interested in Sheriff, like, did he instruct me to do so, or is he in contact with you guys? I was confused at that, and then Rob started shouting and swearing," said Regina, who seemed to be feeling better.

"You write an email to the Board and appraise them about Rob's ruthless behavior. In the meantime, we will try to find out what is going on between Rob and Sheriff. Is it that they have parted ways?" Olive said, trying to figure out the logic behind their actions.

"Could be possible. In the last meeting, Rob and Sheriff had a fallout. Basically, Rob shouted at Sheriff insanely for reasons I don't know. He even accused Sheriff of plotting against him to get the presidency of the Club," said Regina.

"OK, now it seems to make sense. They are not together anymore. Considering Joshua, the Board president, is Sheriff's friend, Rob might be feeling uneasy and is trying to harass people to get some information, which might work against Sheriff. Regina, this is the best time for us. Write an email now to the Board. I am certain Joshua will be more than willing to act against Rob," Olive remarked, trying to put the puzzle pieces correctly.

Regina's email proved to be the last straw. Joshua was very sensitive against workplace harassment; hence, he was in no mood to let Rob go easily.

"Rob, what is going on? I just received an email from Ms. Regina. She accused you and Ellis of harassment. Is it true?" Joshua questioned Rob, full of anger.

Rob tried to reason but couldn't come up with an appropriate answer. Consequently, Joshua dissolved the governing board and Rob's presidency with immediate effect. While he was passing orders over the phone, his secretary typed the email. The content of the official communique further included an increase in directors from 4 to 5 so that a simple majority could vote the president out, instructions for interested members to register themselves as candidates within a week, and an announcement regarding the least number of candidates for the presidency, if there were less than two candidates, the Board reserved the right appoint a new president, the email said.

The voting process was similar to the parliamentary system. Members were to vote for six directors, who then chose a president among themselves. Thus, the governing board would include five directors and a president. Presidential candidates were allowed to vote for themselves.

The governing board's dissolution opened the door for political wrangling within the Club. While everyone was certain of Olive's win, Rob was not willing to go down without a fight. He submitted his papers and asked 5 of his loyal members to submit their applications for directorship, including Ellis. He still fantasized about having the required number to make it to the top. *Only recently, the majority had voted for the ruling and me, which sidelined Like-Minded, and they will trust me again,* thought Rob. He, however, was discounting the Sheriff -Joshua effect. Earlier, he got the votes because of his power and backing from the Board. This time, though, he was alone and without the presidential powers. More importantly, Olive was the popular leader, the proverbial rising sun. It would be hard for the juniors to overlook one of them and support Rob.

Rob wanted Ellis in because of his strong connection with the team leaders and junior members. He was accessible to all and was the only director with whom everyone felt easy to communicate. More often in the past, members would use Ellis as their spokesperson to forward their demands to the Club's governing board. Rob was banking on Ellis' interpersonal skills and his ability to connect with the people to get elected and provide the required support. While Ellis' forte was his great interpersonal skills, his tendency to jump to conclusions and take everything personally were major drawbacks. Consequently, without realizing he had always held biased opinions and viewed people with opposing ideas as his enemies.

No wonder, over the years, he has formed a good relationship with Rob, another person with a stubborn and inflexible nature.

From the Like-Minded group, Olive submitted her application along with Grace, Alan, Regina, Paul, and Harry for directorship. Olive had coaxed Paul to come out of his solitary life and play a meaningful part in the Club. An old-timer like Paul, one of the founding members, coming back and supporting Olive gave her a big boost. Even senior Unionists respected Paul for all his contributions and were forced to shift their loyalties.

The biggest news was Sheriff contesting the elections as an independent candidate. His act put doubts within the minds of the members. Everyone knew about his diplomatic prowess and strategic mindset. For many, he was the one who ensured stabilization within the Club in the past; otherwise, given Rob's authoritative nature, it would have been difficult to remain in power for so long. More importantly, Sheriff's connections with the Board and the president were well-known. Therefore, the majority viewed him as the main driving force behind Rob's time in power. With Sheriff out of the camp, Unionists were divided, severely denting Rob's vote bank.

March 31, 2021, was the last date for the candidates to submit their papers. Once it passed, the Board announced the election date and named an interim governing board to oversee all the matters. Electronic voting was introduced for transparency; the head office sent the machines to avoid the last-minute hassle of purchasing new ones. Plus, the management didn't want another conspiracy to rear its head. However, the biggest decision was to do away with the president's veto power. Without a simple majority of the directors' votes, no changes in rules could be possible. A rule that would come to haunt Olive badly in the coming years.

Chapter Five: Mirage in the Desert

The voting was scheduled for eleven in the morning. Early by Mathew's standard, considering that it was Sunday as well. However, looking at his wife, he decided to drop her off. But on one condition.

"How rude, Mat. Here I am, feeling nervous, and you are planning to eat out. So unfair! You could at least wait for me to come back." Olive was clearly not pleased with her husband's plans.

"We can go out again, honey. No problem from our side. The Breakfast Klub is just a 5-minute drive away from your club; you don't expect me to come home without going there, do you?"

"Yes, I do."

"Sadly, dear, you are mistaken," Mathew said with a straight face. "Come on. I know you're gonna win;

think of it as your pre-victory celebration. I will send you the pics."

"Shut up, Mat. And look at this," Olive said while poking at her husband's bulging tummy. "You promised to reduce."

"From Monday, honey."

"Mom, just one more day," Jonathan, Olive's younger son, pleaded, making a cute puppy face.

"Like father like son."

"Yes. Hurry up, Jimmy. Otherwise, we will leave you," Mathew called out his elder son and went out. He didn't want to delay, or Olive might change her mind. She couldn't be blamed either; he had promised Olive to start working out more than a year back. Looking at his belly, he thought, *Olive is right. I need to reduce; I will start tomorrow.*

Mathew dropped off Olive at the Club's office and headed off to the family's favorite restaurant to enjoy brunch with their kids. It was a sedate Sunday morning in Houston. The temperature was in the late eighties, with a lovely breeze. And it showed as more and more people headed to the beaches to enjoy the beautiful weather. Everyone seemed to be in the vacation mood, apart from Olive. She was twitchy and sweating profusely. Though she has hyperhidrosis—a condition that makes a person sweat heavily—her current state even surpassed that.

At the parking lot, Olive's team was waiting for her. They all looked pumped up and ready for the action.

"Hello, Madam to-be President," Grace called out. "Well, how that sounds? Madam President… this will certainly be the first for me," she asked others.

"First of all, it's presidentess and not madam president, though people use it. Secondly, it sounds perfect to me. It is about time we start hearing presidentess or madam president more often; mister president is old-fashioned and has outlived its expiry date. Not saying that men shouldn't be presidents anymore, but only if merited," Harry said, coming forward to shake hands with Olive.

"We have a feminine for president? Didn't know that," Grace looked surprised.

"Girl, you need to work on your vocabulary," Alan teased her. Hearing that, they all laughed.

Olive badly needed that conversation just to calm her nerves down. She was feeling anxiously excited, with more tilted toward anxiousness.

"Come on, let's go; the voting is gonna start," Regina shouted from behind.

***

Last week was a roller-coaster ride for all the parties concerned. Time passed at a breakneck speed, with every minute being an event. Joshua didn't want any untoward event to occur; hence, he instructed the interim to remain extra vigilant. Being linked with the Rob and Sheriff duo was beginning to be a nuisance. Even the Board's supreme council members were voicing their concern for the mudslinging it caused to the post of the highest authority. Therefore, he wanted things to be done and dusted as soon as possible in a transparent manner. Siding with any candidate was the last thing on Joshua's mind, considering the leverage it would provide to his opponent on the Board's presidential elections. It was the classic example of everyone trying to save their backsides. Given the notoriety with which the Board and Club were managed under the Joshua-Rob nexus, it was bound to happen. The only question was when.

Olive's firm stand against Rob's provided the disgruntled members a rallying platform to raise their voices in unison without the fear of being singled out. Getting sidelined by the people of their own ilk wouldn't inspire many junior members, especially in a foreign land where the association is the biggest and often the only reference. Consequently, Olive's stance gained more prominence and importance. The kind of vigor and passion it instilled in the Club's members were something to behold. *I haven't seen this enthusiasm since James' days,* Paul thought. *Who would have thought that a junior affiliate would arouse such a response and that, too, a lady? Well, things are changing fast, for sure.*

Paul greatly respected Olive's leadership. She was a visionary leader who believed in taking everyone along. Her words had motivated all the members, senior or junior, and forced them to come out of their cocooned lives to play a more productive role for the Club and their country at large. For once, they were not afraid of Rob's authority.

However, does she possess the diplomatic nuance and policy-making ingenuity to undo the wrong of the last ten years? This question has created doubt in Paul's vis-a-vis Olive's ability to deliver the goods. Despite her contribution to the Club, Paul didn't view her as an ideal candidate for the presidency. In his view, sloganeering could get the ground support, but it required an experienced and calmer head to achieve the results.

"In the end, it is the results that matter," Paul opined in front of the Like-Minded group. "We all are qualified accountants and know very well the importance of a favorable bottom line. You will not sustain for long if you are not achieving your targets, no matter how good you are."

Paul's words, though insightful, created doubt among the Like-Minded members. Some started favoring him for the presidential spot simply because of his seniority and services to the Club, while some were of the view that Olive, being a lady, was susceptible to emotional outbreaks, which could be devastating for the organization and herself also. The remaining supported Olive and resolved to stand by her. They suspected Paul of eyeing the presidency and blamed him for sowing a discording seed among the members to achieve personal ambitions. Upon hearing Paul's views and sensing a potentially destructive divide, Olive advised that whoever secured the greater number of votes would be the presidential candidate.

Her recommendation did manage to silence the diverging voices; however, it proved to be a stop-gap arrangement only. The worst was to follow.

While they may not be intended to, Paul's words favored Rob and the Unionists most. Upon hearing about the division among the ranks of his opponents, Rob quickly called Ellis and instructed him to spread negative propaganda against Olive.

"Paul has just shown us the way, Ellis, try to make the most of it. Call our members and tell them to spread gender-based disinformation directed at Olive. She wants equal representation for women; let's show her what we men have to endure."

"Hahaha. Rob, you could shame even the most evil of them all," Ellis replied. "I will pass the instructions immediately and ensure they are adhered to the fullest."

"Ellis, is it possible to talk to the Like-Mindeds?" Rob asked.

"Let me see," was all Ellis could muster. He was unsure how to get the Like-Minded to attend their gathering.

"Dear fellow accountants, how are you all? I am sure you must be wondering why we called you here. Basically, we have been thinking about our association for the last one week. Yes, we have made some mistakes over the years and are willing to rectify our course. Therefore, we ask you to believe in us and our abilities. Remember, we safely negotiated our club from the days of the Great Recession and COVID-19 and made sure young accountants like you get good jobs. More importantly, what does the Like-Minded have to offer? Do they have a record to show their expertise in running an organization? No! Secondly, their leadership is not united. It is they who are chasing their personal dreams and are accusing us of doing so. We believe Paul and Olive's diverging views should alarm you about their lack of planning in running this organization. In the end, we would like to thank you for taking out some time and coming here. We are greatly honored."

Though Rob had always been a great orator, what set this speech apart from the others was the calculated use of we. He tried to sound inclusive while portraying his opponents as alienating and disjointed. The move seemed to work.

***

Sheriff spent the last week thinking about his plan of action. He had both options available to him: either rejoin the Rob group or lend his support to Olive.

Hearing that Sheriff had submitted his papers as an independent candidate, Olive and other Like-Minded people contacted him to learn more about his position. Though they didn't explicitly express their desire for his support, he could make out what they were looking for. Sheriff had been brilliant in reading between the lines. It provided him with more maneuverable space than he had initially expected. However, he was unsure of the general sentiment within the Like-Minded camp. Yes, he was approached, but nothing concrete had been communicated to him. Like always, he didn't want to commit before knowing the true intentions of his opponents.

Though not many Like-Minded members were positive about getting in touch with Sheriff, Olive was of the opinion that his experience of working as a director and contacts within the Board would be of great help. It was a marked shift from her previous position. Earlier, she opposed all the Unionists, labeling them corrupt and avaricious.

"No doubt, Sheriff is not a clean guy, but we can make good use of his expertise. None of us has the complete picture of how the Club has been managed for the last three years or so. Therefore, having an insider with us will help our team to negotiate the initial period in case we win the elections."

Olive's suggestion was based on pragmatism and provided insight into how she was planning to manage the Club. Olive initially believed in conforming to her ideals by trying to onboard members, if not finding alternatives, and eventually taking a solo flight. It has brought her success in the past as a professional but also has painted a negative picture of her as someone afraid of making decisions on her own, though nothing could be farther from the truth than that.

Basically, it was not totally her idea. Paul was also supportive of reaching out to Sheriff.

"Yes, we know he was Rob's right hand and had been involved, either directly or indirectly, in all his wrongdoings, but this doesn't mean that Sheriff is not something who can manage things well. I would say having him on our side will only bode well for us. Moreover, we will monitor his working, and in case he is found to be indulging in corrupt activities, he will be shown the door right away. All I am suggesting is that, in order to redo the system, we will require someone who initially created it. Plus, Sheriff is alone now and doesn't have much influence, so we can get him to follow our conditions easily."

"This is not the ideologue Paul I know talking. What has happened to you, old man?" Harry's sarcastic question probed his old friend.

"I just got wiser, my friend," Paul replied plainly.

"We shall see, Paul; we shall see," Harry grunted.

On the other hand, Ellis had persuaded Rob to negotiate with Sheriff.

"Rob, you know we need him more than he needs us. I believe we should contact him and ask him to support us. You can't deny that Sheriff has a following; many young accountants look up to him. Even if he is uncomfortable joining us, we may ask him to instruct his people to vote for our candidates and later support our policies in the governing board."

"How can you be so sure that Sheriff will win?" asked Rob.

"Rob, I have been in constant contact with members more than any of the directors. Despite all the negative rumors, Sheriff is popular among them.

His friendship with Joshua is also a factor. You just can't do away with him, not in the short-term," Ellis elucidated.

"But I am not doing it. I have had enough of this back-stabbing fox," shouted Rob.

"OK, I will talk to him. Promise me that you won't create a scene if he agrees to my plan."

"Do as you please."

"No, Rob, promise me," demanded Ellis in a firm voice.

"Yeah, yeah, I promise not to interfere." Rob knew it was not the right time to argue with Ellis. Moreover, he just wanted to win at any cost. And like always with Rob, the end justified the means even if he has to reconcile with Sheriff, momentarily.

After getting Rob's confirmation, Ellis spoke to Sheriff and tried to win back his support. However, he didn't get what he was looking for. Citing Rob's obnoxious behavior since that meeting, Sheriff didn't promise much apart from "will consider the offer."

For Sheriff, though, the waiting game continued.

***

The voting day didn't go as expected. Turnout was below par; it seemed the confusion among the members kept them away from voting. It surprised the Like-Minded group no end. They were not expecting such a lukewarm response, at least not from the junior members. During the election campaign, Like-Minded people had contacted all the listed members of the Club and were confident that at least sixty-five percent of the voters would exercise their right. It was not to be. The final figures showed that roughly thirty-five percent of members showed up on that day.

If the voter turnaround was a surprise for the Like-Minded, the results gave an even bigger shock. Of the six candidates, only three won. Olive, Paul, and Harry secured their seats as directors from the Like-Minded group, while Ellis, Rob, and Sheriff also won. Rob barely managed to secure enough votes to make the cut. Though it came as a rude reality check for him, he was happy that Olive didn't win the clear majority. She needed three votes from the governing board to become the president but only had 2. Everything hinged on Sheriff's vote; by the stroke of luck, he was again the kingmaker.

According to the Board's directive, winning directors need to choose a president within a week. The interim governing board set June 11, 2021, as the date for the presidential election. The candidates were Olive and Rob. Though Rob didn't have any chance to win, he was hell-bent on denying Olive the opportunity. *No freaking woman would rule over my club,* he thought. Immediately, he instructed Ellis to contact Sheriff and ask him to vote for Rob. With his vote, Rob would have three votes, equal to Olive's; Harry and Paul were assured to vote for her. The impasse would force the Board to go for reelection, allowing Rob and Ellis more time to eke out some more support from the members.

Meanwhile, it would dent the notion of Olive being a popular leader.

For the Like-Minded, assured of their victory, the results resulted in chaos among the ranks. Members were finger-pointing each other to pass on the blame for the supposed loss. The huge gulf between expectations and reality was too much for most to handle. Harry was first to blame Olive for the unexpected result.

"You met with Sheriff. It sent a bad signal to our voters; they thought we had deviated from our manifesto. Thus, they decided to abstain from voting. Look at the figures; the young voters' percentage is so low. Whether you accept it or not, you are the reason."

"Harry, calm down and think rationally. This is not a time for infighting," Paul tried to cool down the temper.

"Oh, come on, Paul. You are equally responsible. You told her to reach out to Sheriff. Now look where we are standing. And Sheriff has the upper hand. He is the kingmaker and can ask for whatever he wants," Harry blurted out again.

"Harry, for Christ's sake, shut up. We are not living in a vacuum. We are not living in an ideal world. Do you think with all their connections, Rob and Sheriff would not have support among the members? And Ellis was the most connected among all the directors. For once, think realistically, considering all the factors on the ground," Paul, for once, lost his temper.

"I'm with Harry. He is right; Olive should not have met with Sheriff. It gave our supporters a wrong impression," Alan called out.

"Me, too," Grace joined in.

"OK, what do you guys want me to do? If Sheriff doesn't support me in the presidential elections, the Board will have to go for reelection. If you want that, I will go for it. But it will further dent our position," Olive advised.

"I agree with her," Paul said. "Anyone with a better option?" he asked.

Silence engulfed the room. Everyone looked out of ideas; they just didn't know what to do or say.

"We don't have eternity to decide; say something," Paul was getting frustrated. He was finding it hard to believe that professionals could be so childish in their approach to think that whatever they had expected would happen in reality. "This is the real world; here, not every time, things will happen according to our whims and fancies," he said as he left the room.

Harry, despite his early burst out, agreed to talk with Sheriff to get Olive elected as president. Alan and Grace, though, didn't change their opinion and left the meeting halfway through.

Ellis tried hard to coax Sheriff back to the Unionist group. He even asked some of Sheriff's close accomplices to make him reconsider his decision, but to no avail. Sheriff was not yielding and had a valid reason for that.

Knowing that Olive couldn't become the president without his support, he decided to vote for her but on his terms. He didn't want to let go of the opportunity once again be the linchpin of the governing board. However, there was another factor that affected his favor. Olive's passion and resilience had impressed him. The way a young lady fought for ideals in a secluded men's club was praiseworthy. For once, a shrewd tactician like Sheriff was overawed. He detested Rob because he misused his talent. On the other hand, Olive was genuinely concerned about the goodwill of her peers and wanted to facilitate them. Therefore, he, for once, decided to give ideals a chance as far as they didn't encroach on his space.

With such high hopes, Sheriff planned to meet Olive and her Like-Minded colleagues. The meeting was planned at Navy Blue with Alan, Grace, Harry, Olive, Paul, Sheriff, and Regina in attendance. He knew Harry and Paul, so he was not surprised by listening to their views and aspirations. Though Paul has toned down a bit, Harry has remained the same. *The same old revolutionary trying to change the world on his own,* Sheriff smirked.

Sheriff was, however, most interested in listening to Olive's perspective. He wanted to know what she was thinking and how she planned to take things forward. And he was not disappointed. Her dedication and devotion to the cause moved him. *Just as I thought.* Olive came across as an irrepressible yet grounded soul who wouldn't compromise on her ideals but was respectful nonetheless.

Others disappointed Sheriff. They were a bunch of indisciplined people who could easily be manipulated and exploited to work against their own people or group. Their ideals and principles were subservient to their emotions. Therefore, they posed the biggest threat to Olive, even bigger than Rob.

The meeting lasted roughly an hour, and Sheriff had arrived at his final decision.

"Young lady, I know working with you will be a challenge as some of our views don't converge, but I like you for your courage and stand. I respect you and am willing to work with you for the betterment of the Club. But I have a word of advice for you: choose your partners wisely. Some of you may view my words skeptically, but these are out of genuine concern. Lastly, I will work with you until I feel your group is behind you. After that, we will part ways. I am telling you beforehand so you won't complain later on."

"Do you think any of us will leave Olive?" Alan asked rather sarcastically.

"I can make out a person when I see one, son."

Sheriff's words left everyone puzzled, but their reality started to dawn upon Olive a couple of months into her presidency. After assuming the office, when she decided to make some changes, the fiercest opposition was from within. This allowed Rob and Ellis to pressurize her even more and portray her image as an inefficient and undeserving leader among the members.

Chapter Six: The Betrayal

Going back to her home after the dinner, Sheriff's words echoed in Olive's mind. She had heard about certain people's uncanny ability to read into others' personalities by observing their body language, like hand gestures, talking style and tone, and facial expressions. However, she hadn't met any individual who could guess so accurately. Sheriff's cautionary message perfectly described her mates after what she had witnessed in the pre and post-election Like-Minded meetings. The uproar created on trivial matters by those Olive trusted and thought were honest to the cause had forced her to consider exercising maximum caution. *Is he a mind reader or has inside news,* she thought. *Whatever the case may be, I need to be vigilant.*

Mathew realized Olive was not her usual chirpy self and seemed lost.

"I believe your meeting with Sheriff didn't go as planned."

"No, it is not that. However, the discussion has posed more questions without answering many."

"Like?"

Olive shared the whole situation, Sheriff's advice, and the condition. Also, the unusual behavior of her group members she had observed recently. Mathew didn't like what he heard but decided to play down the matter to not make her uncomfortable.

"It's way past our bedtime; you look sleepy, probably that's why reading too much into it," he replied calmly and walked her to bed.

Olive kept quiet but knew something was amiss. She dearly wanted Mathew to be right; *maybe I was overthinking due to tiredness*. She assured herself and went to sleep.

***

Though Like-Minded got the majority, with Sheriff joining them in the governing body, Paul was not entirely happy with the outcome. For him, it was the last chance to become president and imitate his idol, James. Alas, it was not to be, all because of Olive. His old ideologue gave way to a power-hungry patriarch who looked down upon a woman despite all her talents and qualities.

"Harry, this is our organization. We built it, and now a youngster will be running it," he complained.

"You feeling jealous?" Harry asked. He was surprised at Paul's behavior. "You should be happy that an idealist like us, who believes in transparency, is at the helm."

"I am happy Rob is no longer the president, but Olive is no match for Rob and Ellis' connivance. She doesn't know how to deal with people and manage things. That's why I believe a senior hand should look after the affairs of the Club. With our slim majority, she will be susceptible to Unionist's trickeries; you know what I mean."

"Why am I getting this feeling that you are feeling awkward to be led by a junior, that too a woman?"

"Hah, women. They only make noises but can't do anything. Olive will also prove to be the same," Paul retorted.

"Don't pass your judgment so early, my friend. Let her showcase her competency, and then we will decide," Harry said, trying to end the conversation. He was clearly getting frustrated.

"When will you come out of that reactionary mode, Harry? You have to realize there won't be another time. If you don't get our act now, Rob and Ellis will not allow us another chance."

"Olive worked hard for the position she has achieved. You were not even active. It was she who got you involved, and now you are planning against her?" Harry got up and started to leave.

"Harry, I am not plotting against her. I am just saying that she is not ready at the moment," Paul toned down, realizing Harry was not buying his point. "This is our first time; thus, the most competent and experienced should take charge, not one of the juniors, who has much to learn."

"Look, Paul, it was decided, and you agreed that whoever would get more votes would run for the presidency. Olive bagged more, and it was her right. I don't think there is anything to complain about. She may be young, but she is mighty talented and mature. You just can't say bad about her without giving her a chance. Still, if you believe that you deserve the chance, table the matter in front of all and let them decide. Two of us can't decide for the lot. Good night."

Harry stared angrily at Paul and left the room. It was pointless to argue. He was worried because of the defiance in Paul's demeanor.

***

As decided, Olive was nominated for the presidency; the number of votes she had received greatly outnumbered Paul's tally. Rob was the other candidate. The interim president conveyed a session of the newly elected directors of the governing board and asked them to choose the new president. Joshua and other members of the Board's supreme council presided over the process through a live Zoom meeting for a smooth transition. Soon, Olive was announced as the winner, shattering Rob's hopes of getting another shot at the top position. Secretly in his heart, he was praying for Sheriff to vote for him. For Sheriff, though, Rob was a finished case, no longer required, at least for the moment.

After the announcement, Rob looked at Sheriff in disgust and murmured, "You, son of a b***." Then, he turned toward Ellis and asked, "What now? Do you want me to work under a woman?"

"Relax, Rob. I have a hunch this won't go far," replied Ellis. "Look at Paul; does he look happy to you?"

Upon Ellis' inquisition, Rob turned and observed Paul's facial expressions. Though he was clapping, his body language suggested anything but contempt toward his leader.

"Hmm… you are right, Ellis. It certainly doesn't look like everything is OK in the Like-Minded camp."

"Ms. Olive, congratulations on becoming the youngest and first female president of the Club. We hope you will take the organization forward and will further enhance its image. As the President of the Board, I welcome you aboard and expect nothing but the best from you to come good on the trust your fellow members have entrusted you. Similarly, I hope and expect the directors to guide and assist you should you face any difficulty. They all are very experienced, and I am sure will offer sound advice. I would also like to assure you that if you need any support from our side, we are always available and will be happy to be of any assistance. Good luck, Ms. Olive, and looking forward to meeting you soon." Saying that Joshua and other Board directors went offline, leaving Olive and the directors to discuss among themselves their next plan of action.

Olive's appointment calmed Joshua's nerves down. His past involvement with Rob was proving to be too big a bogey for his comfort. He just wanted to come clean on all the allegation charges, and for that, he wanted Rob out of the office. Having a junior affiliate at the helm, and that too a woman, would favor him. Firstly, he could silence the naysayers, spreading rumors that Joshua would rig the elections to get his man to the position. It didn't transpire. Secondly, working with Olive would allow Joshua an opportunity to portray himself as future-oriented and a believer in gender equality. He clearly has emerged as the biggest beneficiary of the whole scenario. For him, it was the perfect time to shed the old skin. Sheriff had forewarned him about Olive and her staunch belief in her ideals, but for now, Joshua was least concerned about that. *Everyone has a price; let the time come.*

***

After assuming the office, Olive's priorities were to start the audit at the earliest and resume the publication of the Club's newsletter. When she tabled the agenda in the governing body's first meeting for approval, there was an uproar. Rob and Ellis opposed the idea, saying that Club was short on cash and should avoid unnecessary expenditures.

"What is the point in publishing the newsletter?" Rob asked.

"We promised transparency to our members. And it means informing them about the working of the Club. Hence, I believe the newsletter is important. It is a way to communicate with all the affiliates and appraise them about what is happening in the organization. Plus, with all the ads, it can also be a source of income," Olive replied.

"Send them all an email if you want to inform them," Rob said nonchalantly. "The expense incurred in publishing a newsletter exceeds the revenue; it's not feasible."

"Emails have very low connectivity as compared to a newsletter. And, if marketed properly, it can be a good source of income. Lastly, a fundraising event is coming up. We can use it to finance this edition of the newsletter. "

Olive was not willing to go down. She knew why Rob and Ellis were opposing newsletter publication. The more people would know about the alleged corruption by the governing body, the more they would reconsider their affiliation with Unionists. She intended to highlight the irregularities of the previous board through the newsletter and the consequent action the Board took. The publication was one way of reaching out to all the members, especially those non-active members who hadn't participated in any of the Club's events for more than a year.

"Why are you after the newsletter? Don't we have anything else to do? Is it that important? Can't we discuss something else?" Ellis called out. He deliberately spoke loudly to divert the attention of his audience. "Paul, Harry, are we here for some newsletter? Can't we talk about more important matters, like audit? Tell me, Olive, how do you plan to get the audit done as instructed by the Board? Do you have any plans?"

Ellis' outburst put Olive off-guard. She paused for a while to think about what to reply, but Paul preceded her.

"Olive, clearly, your obsession with the newsletter is uncalled for. This is governing board's first meeting, and you are raising such trivial matters."

"Paul, transparency is two-pronged: financial and informational. Members should know what is happening here," Olive replied sternly. She didn't expect her old guard to turn up against her. "We need to keep the people updated. I can safely vouch that some wouldn't even know that Like-Minded are in power now."

"But it is not the first priority," Paul responded.

"I had emailed Joshua regarding the audit, asking for some clarification and more time. He replied that he would be in Houston in a week's time and would discuss the matter in person."

"So you didn't deem it necessary to discuss that with us?" Rob almost jumped from his seat.

"What was there to discuss with you?" Olive was startled.

"Before writing that email, you should have informed us. Under new conditions, you can't make decisions on your own; you need our permission."

"But I was not deciding about anything…I just needed some clarification!"

"Still. You should have informed us," Ellis joined in.

He and Rob could sense the kill and wanted to take full advantage of the situation. Paul had openly voiced his disagreement, which also provided a lifeline to Unionists. Olive was down, with one less support, and the two wanted to keep her there.

"I told you it won't last long," whispered Ellis.

"Yeah…keep it going," Rob said.

"This is such unprofessional behavior, unlike a president. I will write an email to Joshua, informing him that our president doesn't find it necessary to discuss important matters with us. Instead, she raises flimsy issues at directors' meetings." Ellis said and left the room, followed by Rob.

Paul looked at Harry and said, "What do you have to say to that, now!" His scathing tone was enough to convey the message that he was right in his assertion about Olive. Harry just shrugged his shoulder without saying a word. No one had imagined that the first session would be marred by the uproar. They both left the room, leaving Olive holding her head with her hands.

"We need to put the matter in front of the group to come up with a befitting reply to Rob and Ellis. We just can't allow them to dictate terms to us," Harry said before leaving.

Meanwhile, Sheriff silently observed all the proceedings. *Oh boy, this ship is sinking even before setting sail,* he thought. He was surprised by Paul's behavior. *An ideologue like him was not supposed to act like that; is something cooking?*

Olive looked at him as if to ask what I did wrong.

"Welcome to the big boys' world, young lady. Here, even the slightest of slips gets punished severely. I hope you will learn something out of this." As Sheriff got up to leave, he patted her and said, "Have courage; this has happened to the best. It is how you come out of it which will define your legacy."

Things couldn't have started worse than this for Olive. Stunned, she picked up her purse and car keys and left for her home. On the way back, her brain replayed every minute of the meeting multiple times. The most hurtful was Paul's indifferent behavior. Not in her wildest dreams has Olive ever imagined that he would desert her like this, especially in front of Rob and Ellis and for such a trivial matter.

"What did I do wrong? I was just asking for permission to restart newsletter publication."

She asked herself this question many times but couldn't come up with a reasonable answer.

Mathew was standing on the balcony when Olive parked her car. He was talking to one of his colleagues about the presentation when he saw her coming out of the car. Her dropped shoulders and labored steps informed him that something was seriously wrong; she seemed to be dragging herself toward the door as if carrying heavy weights. He immediately disconnected the call and waited for Olive to come up.

"Hi, honey. Is everything OK?" Mathew asked, handing Olive a glass of her favorite strawberry juice.

"Yes, Mat. I am a bit tired and want to sleep, please. Sorry," was all Olive could say.

She didn't want to show her pain to Mathew, fearing that he may react negatively. She really loved him and didn't want to feel bad about anything concerning her.

"Olive, are you sure you are OK? You can share it with me," Mathew tried again.

Hearing that, she ran to Mathew, hugged him tightly, and told him everything.

"Mat, tell me, what was my mistake?"

"Olive, your biggest was that you have challenged the status quo. Being a junior female accountant, you didn't have any right to raise your voice against the big boys, those who have been calling all the shots. For such a big mistake, no blunder, you have to face the punishment, and it will be severe. They will make you an example so that no other junior or a woman dear to question their decisions."

"Why are you frightening me, Mat?"

"Just telling you the reality."

"So."

"You have only two choices: either stay strong or surrender. Make your pick."

"OK, Mat."

Chapter Seven: Incompetence or Inexperience

We all have that one quality we admire the most (Well, some self-obsessed people like everything about themselves, but we are not talking about them.). That one quality, it can be a talent or a skill, defines us; in a way, it gives us identification and makes us confident and prominent among others. Its presence is felt the most when one is pushed against the wall. That's when it manifests itself in the most striking manner and proves to be a lifesaver.

Likewise, one personal strength that Olive liked was her capability to come out of a difficult situation quickly. She believed life was too short to be carrying all the burdens of the past. Thus, in order to live happily and peacefully, one should always look ahead with a positive demeanor. However, it didn't mean not recognizing and owning one's mistakes. For Olive, it meant moving forward after learning from them, trying not to commit them again. She followed a tried and tested procedure, which she had developed over the years, whenever faced with a difficulty or an awkward situation after committing a mistake. First, recognize the root cause that prompted the mistake. Second, analyze all the contexts and the mistakes committed. Third, try to rectify it.

Life for Olive hadn't come easy. Belonging to a middle-class family from a developing Asian country, she had limited opportunities. However, not the one to lay down easily, Olive tried to carve a destiny of her own and chose a career erstwhile considered to be for men only; chartered accountancy. There was opposition and pressure to reconsider her choice; she remained firm. Despite her academic success, there were always dissenting voices judging her and passing their remarks for stepping out of societal boundaries and daring to be different. To counter all those obnoxious comments and behaviors, Olive devised a procedure of her own to preserve her mental health. For her, her immediate family mattered the most, and since they were supportive, others didn't matter; they weren't that important to be taken seriously.

This recognize, analyze, and rectify model proved helpful in her professional life as well. As she grew into her career and her managerial skills were called into practice, Olive, more often than not, would rely on her method to bail her out. Over the years, she had gotten used to it so much that it had invariably become her part, her second nature.

***

Sunday, August 15, 2021. Olive was up early for the monthly general members' meeting. The last two months since assuming the presidency had been challenging, not allowing her enough time to interact with junior affiliates. This time, though, she was determined to make the most of the opportunity to meet them and get to know about their issues and demands. Deep down, she was feeling guilty, as if she had betrayed them. Her idea of being close to the members was proving rather elusive.

She was ahead of schedule, so decided to prepare herself coffee. She looked out of the balcony and marveled at some of the engineering wonders. She was lost in the view when Mathew joined her.

"Morning."

"Morning. Up early today?"

"Yeah. Off late, not getting much time to talk to you, so I thought this would be the best time, madam president."

"Since when you became so formal, Mat?"

"Since you decided to act differently."

"Meaning?"

"Don't you get bored acting like a president all the time, even at home? Look at yourself in the mirror and ask is the presidency worth it?"

"Mat...."

"I know you take your association with the Club very seriously, but at what cost, Olive?"

"What's your point, Mat?"

Olive was clearly confused by Mathew's behavior. He was acting strangely and was not himself.

"Do we have some time?"

"Yes."

"How much?"

"Mat, why are you going in circles? Come to the point. You are driving me crazy now. You know it is a general members' meeting today, and I am a bit nervous as it is." She complained, venting her frustration at him for not comprehending her situation and behaving like a spoilsport.

"My point exactly, Olive."

"Here we go again, Mat. What's the point of all this?"

"Look at your last couple of months, Olive. How much time do you have for us?"

"Mat, you know I have just been elected as the president of the Club, and the responsibilities demand my attention and time there. Don't think that is so difficult to understand."

"Agree. But what about your family? Don't we deserve your time and attention?"

"This is not the time to get sentimental, Mat."

"I am not, Olive. I am just reminding you that you have a family as well." Saying that he got up and left.

Olive followed him into the room.

"You mean I am overlooking you guys?" she asked.

"Yes."

"You know I am a bit tied up. Just give me some time, and everything will be back to normal."

"No, it won't."

"What do you mean?"

"Olive, from where I am looking, the way you are handling things, it won't get any easier."

"And?"

"You have taken it upon yourself to do everything on your own. That's not how associations or organizations work, Olive. I know I am not a president of some club, but being a project manager, I know how to handle things. And the way you are doing it, that's bound to fail."

"I am listening, Mat."

"Olive, being a president doesn't mean you need to do everything yourself. This way, you will only tire yourself, and the end result will be zero despite all your efforts. You wouldn't achieve anything like this because, as a person, you can't perform everything. All your and you're your team's hard work will count for nothing. Plus, this will demotivate the people willing to contribute. They will consider you an I-know-it-all boss who is always poking her nose into everything. Do you want that? Alienating people from yourself will only help your opponents.

"Olive, I know your intentions are noble, and you genuinely want to help your fellow accountants, but your execution is not how it should be. If you will keep yourself busy with menial day-to-day tasks, how will you manage the overall working of the Club? Learn to delegate and supervise."

Then it clicked with Olive. Indeed, she had been fretting needlessly over matters that didn't require her attention and time as the president. Instead, they could have easily been tackled by the team leaders. However, there was a reason.

"Mat, maybe what you are saying is correct. I tried giving people responsibilities, but I found them unresponsive."

"Olive, it has been just two months since you took charge. How can you judge so quickly? And, if you think that junior members are not willing, talk to them, and if their lazy attitude continues, change them. You doing their work is not the answer. Think of your Club as a company. If any of your team members don't perform, will you start working on their behalf? No. You talk to them, caution them, and lastly, fire them.

Similarly, in the Club also: talk to them, caution them, and then relieve them of their responsibilities. I know team members are working only as volunteers and don't make any money, but getting recognition is a very strong incentive. Incentivize their work. You know any recognition from an association like yours can go a long way in enhancing professional growth prospects; employers value such employees.

"Work smartly, madam president. Hard work alone will not get you the desired results. I am not questioning your competence, nor am I suggesting that since you don't have any experience, you can't manage it. I am just asking you to do some course correction."

Mathew's words forced Olive to ponder. There was no denying the fact that she was getting involved with way too many things, which were delaying more important matters. Last month, when Joshua visited the Club, he had instructed Olive to present to him her plan of conducting the pending audit of the Club. He had instructed her to expedite the issue since it had been pending for long. However, due to her preoccupation, she hasn't been able to complete the presentation.

"Olive," Mathew continued, "today is your general meeting. Do you think one person can look after all the matters? No, that's why we make teams and appoint a team leader responsible for discharging the assigned tasks efficiently and effectively."

She stared at her cup, not knowing what to say. All the events of the last two months flashed before her eyes. Mathew realized that his wife had a lot on her mind. Something she had been holding on to prevent their home environment from deteriorating. He walked up to her and said, "No matter what, Olive, you can always count on me for support."

Olive hugged Mathew tightly and buried her head in his arms. For once, she didn't want to go to the Club. She wanted to remain there with Mathew and not be concerned about anything.

"Mat, I didn't realize how much I had hurt you and our sons," she said apologetically.

"It's OK, Olive."

"I devoted all my weekends to the Club when it was you guys I should be spending time with."

"Olive, I am not against you working for the Club. I was just against the manner. You were taking too much undue stress. As a result, I was losing the real Olive. I respect your feelings about doing social work, but not at the cost of losing your identity. If you promise me to remain the same Olive I loved, you are free to work at the Club; we have no qualms."

"Mat, I will not change. I promise," Olive said tearfully and nuzzled her face on his chest.

"At what time was your meeting?" Mathew asked.

"Earlier, you wanted me to stay, and now you are asking me to go?" Olive questioned.

"I love you, Olive. I will never stop you from realizing your dreams because I know how much you have worked hard for them. But I will also not want you to change. I just want the same Olive I married."

"I love you, too, Mat."

"Too much emotional talk for a day. If you want to attend the meeting, fix yourself. I will be waiting for you downstairs."

"Thanks, Mat."

***

Saturday, July 17, 2021. After assuming the office, Olive appointed Paul as the head to supervise the audit of the Club. However, he excused himself.

"Paul, the audit of Club was the heart and soul of the Like-Minded movement because it was the best way to maintain transparency. You had always raised your voice for that. And now today, when I am asking you to supervise it, you are saying no. any specific reason?"

"Olive, I don't think I will be able to manage it well. I have some family issues to manage. Hence, I won't be able to give time."

"Is that all, Paul? If something is bothering you, share it with me."

"Nothing, Olive. I just need some time to spend with my family," came the reply from Paul.

"OK."

"Anything else, Olive?"

"No, that would be it. Kindly send Harry in. I will ask him to manage the audit."

"Sure."

Paul left the room and went to find Harry. He was in the meeting room, exchanging views with their newly-appointed team leaders. Paul called Harry aside and updated him about the matter.

"Olive wanted me to head the audit committee, but now that I am not in, she wants you to take the task."

Harry didn't like the way Paul communicated; he felt insulted.

"Olive, you called me?" Harry asked before entering her office.

"Yes, Harry. I wanted you to head the audit committee. As per Joshua's instructions, I want to start it as soon as possible, and I think you will be the most suitable guy. Please go through the accounts and update me on how much time and human resources you would require. I will ask Joseph to give you access to all the accounts records for the last five years."

"Most suitable guy. I believe you can save that for Paul."

"Pardon."

"You offered him the role first, right?"

"Harry, you and Paul are the same for me, and you know that. I have always respected you two for being the founding members of the Club. I initially believed you would be better suited to train the young team leaders to manage the workload because of your close relationship. Now that Paul has backed out, I don't think there is any better person to supervise the audit than you."

"Olive, you must understand that Paul was against your nomination for the presidency. He maintained that you, being a woman, were not suitable to lead the Club, and it was I who supported you. Still, you favored him?" Harry's scathing comment came as a big surprise for her.

"Harry, it is not like that. I just…."

"It is OK, Olive. It is a timely reminder for me how much our leadership values me. It is almost evening now; I will contact Joseph tomorrow and will check the records."

Olive couldn't believe what she was hearing. Paul and Harry, the two stalwarts of the Club and her biggest support…were lost. And they were supposed to be the ideologues who favored Like-Minded because Olive and her group stood for transparency. She unlocked her system and sent an email to all the directors, informing them about Harry's appointment as the leader of the audit team.

The next morning, Rob and Ellis barged into her room.

"What is the meaning of your email, Olive?" Rob shouted.

"What?" Olive replied.

"You can't simply appoint Harry as the head; he is a member of your group."

"So?"

"We demand equal representation of both the groups. One from Like-Minded and one from the Unionists," Rob demanded.

"I am afraid you are not in the position," Olive replied irritatingly.

"Yes, we are. As governing board members, we are," Ellis joined in. "If you don't announce Rob as a co-head of the audit team, we will send an email to the

Board's president, asking him to intervene. After the new laws, you can't decide on your own without our approval."

They both left, and soon Olive received an email from Rob, cc'ed to Joshua, wherein he accused her of making arbitrary decisions without taking the opposition into confidence. She immediately called the meeting of the Like-Minded to discuss with them the matters at hand.

"Guys, let's meet at the conference room today; I have some developments to share. Everyone, please confirm your availability ASAP. It is a bit urgent and important," Olive texted on the WhatsApp group.

The meeting was scheduled in an hour's time, allowing Olive some space to regroup and recollect her thoughts. When feeling anxious, coffee was her perfect riposte. She left her room and headed to the canteen. It served the perfect coffee, just like she wanted it to be, and on that day, too, it was no different. *How badly I needed it*, she thought while playing her favorite song on YouTube. There weren't many members sitting in the canteen, so Olive didn't have to act formally like a president and could be herself. Half an hour later, she was ready to meet the Like-Minded, feeling fresher and more charged. That was the effect coffee had on her.

All the seats in the conference room got filled as the Like-Minded members made their way in. Olive waited for them to settle down before starting.

"We have a problem on our hands. Rob and Ellis had opposed Harry as the team leader of the Club's audit team. They want representation also. I know this is far-fetched, but they are arguing. Their only point in defense is that, as directors, they should have been informed. Any suggestions?"

"Let's call a directors' meeting and get this sorted out," suggested Paul.

"You are right, Paul, but calling a directors' meeting for such trivial matters will only us slow down. We need to have a permanent solution. This is getting utterly irritating now. There is no sense of ownership left in me. Every time I make a decision, both of them start accusing me. I believe they are just doing it to delay our work so we could be defamed in front of the Board. First, when I talked about the newsletter, they wanted to get things going on the audit, and now this. It is only their ploy to frustrate us."

"What do you want from us? Why don't you call your buddy, Sheriff, and get things sorted in the governing board meeting." The bitterness in Alan's comment showed his disapproval of Olive's earlier decision.

"I have called you all to discuss the matter and devise a comprehensive strategy. Then we will put the matter in front of Sheriff and ask him to support us. Why are you obsessed with him all the time?" Olive was clearly not in the mood to listen to any unjustified grievances. She has had enough.

"Because siding with Sheriff meant going against all our principles. You backstabbed us then, which resulted in this situation," Alan retorted.

"This is not the time to needlessly fight among ourselves. If we want to be productive and achieve our goals, we must look ahead," Olive remarked dismissively.

"I second Alan's point, but I don't think this is the appropriate time to bring up this issue," Harry joined in to diffuse the situation.

"You all want instant results, but it seems no one is willing to help me get through these demanding times. We have to acknowledge that Rob and his cohorts were part of this system for a good 10-12 years. They know it better than anyone and are taking advantage of the loopholes. And instead of helping me to come up with an efficient counterstrategy, all you guys are debating about me meeting with Sheriff. Are you guys even interested in what we set out to do? Or were those slogans merely to get some attention?"

"Now…now…. Relax everyone. Just calm down. We are not doing ourselves any favor fighting like this. Can we, for once, act like mature professionals," Paul spoke. "What Olive is saying about Rob and Ellis is correct, and we need to be serious about it."

"Paul, I don't think you should be lecturing us about being mature after what you were contemplating about Olive," Harry spat.

"Can we, please, just stop pointing fingers, please? I want solutions for the problems Unionists are creating for us. But we are fighting among ourselves. Is this the way we will run this Club? I want you all to stick to the issue, please," Olive pleaded.

"In the short run, the only viable solution is to put the matter in the governing body meeting and get it approved with a majority. Meanwhile, we will try to formulate a comprehensive plan against Rob and Ellis' delaying tactics. That's all from me," Harry said.

"And what about others?" Olive asked. "Any other bright ideas?"

She waited for some moments in case any other member decided to speak up, but nobody came forward.

"OK, then. It seems you all agree with what Harry said, and we will proceed accordingly. Thank you for coming on such short notice."

Olive took her laptop and left the conference room immediately. The meeting was a horror show for her. She couldn't fathom that her friends had such deep grievances with her. *It seems my presidency has created a ridge between us. Instead of supporting me, they are accusing me of deviating from the manifesto,* she thought.

Chapter Eight: The Sinking Ship

"Hello, Olive; how are you? Sorry for the delay. I had promised to come early, but some Board issues kept me busy," Joshua said, coming into the president's office. "I hope you will not judge me for that."

"Hi, Joshua. First of all, welcome to the United States. I am fine; I hope you had a pleasant flight. And no, no… You must have been busy; no one is judging you for the delay," Olive replied with her trademark smile.

Though Olive had seen Joshua before in the Club's meetings, this was the first time she was meeting him in person. His personality and demeanor caught her a bit off guard. Joshua has a calming yet commanding aura about him, which those who were not in close acquaintance with him could find compelling or assertive. He always exuded the feeling of being in control. Plus, the great negotiator he was, he had a way with words and could put even the best of the speakers in a spin.

For a moment or two, Olive was completely overawed by the presence of the Board's president. She was experiencing the typical fanboy moment, getting completely starstruck by Joshua. *Well, he didn't look that handsome from the distance*, she thought. Her amazement was so obvious that even Joshua noticed it.

"Did you say something, Ms Olive?" he asked while sitting at the main table.

"Just want to ask tea or coffee. Heads up: our canteen has the best coffee in Houston." Olive conjured up some words to overcome the disconcerting feeling.

"OK, then coffee it is." Joshua paused for a moment and then continued. "It seems you have altered the office setting. Nice!" He scanned the room with a grateful smile and nodded his head in approval.

"Thanks. Yes, we just shuffled some of the furniture around," replied Olive.

"Well, they say women are more creative when it comes to styling, and it shows. You have revamped the room. It is giving out different vibes."

Joshua was really impressed by what he was seeing. During Rob's tenure, the same room used to be lifeless and dreary, with all dark-colored settings. Now, it seemed spicier and more lively.

"Shuffled; is it not new furniture? I think the color is the same," he was still puzzled as to how Olive managed to pep up the room.

"No. We swapped the directors' room furniture with this one. Its lighter shade contrasted with the darker colors of the room," Olive explained somewhat proudly. The early jitters were gone, and she was feeling confident.

"I must say, you have impressed me with your creative flair and artistic taste, and I hope the same can be said about your leadership. I have heard a lot about you, your dedication and passion, and hence expect much from you. Young leaders like you can take this organization far. This will be great for the juniors and the country as well."

"I appreciate your kind words, Joshua," was all Olive could manage.

The early exchange with Joshua was a welcome relief from the trauma Olive had endured in the previous two weeks. What Rob and Ellis were doing was not unexpected. Being the opposition, they were supposed to create hurdles to delay the progress. She had prepared her mind for that. However, the kind of treatment she received from her own party members was worrisome. They were doubting her abilities and intentions, accusing her of going back on her words to cling to the power. To top it all, an experienced person like Paul didn't consider her worthy at all for the office just because she was a woman. Olive was fighting a lonely battle on multiple fronts.

***

Sunday, July 18, 2021. Olive called Paul, Harry, Alan, and Grace to her room for a meeting.

"Yesterday, we all agreed to table a motion to appoint Harry as the team leader to supervise the Club's internal audit. Alan and Grace, I want you guys to please put it in writing latest by the afternoon so that I may call a governing body meeting next Saturday. I don't want to delay the matter anymore. Otherwise, it will send a wrong message to the Board and will also strengthen the Unionists' narrative of us being incompetent."

"OK."

"Harry and Paul, I have asked Sheriff to come to the office today. I hope he will be coming soon. We will go and appraise him about the matter and will ask him to vote for our motion."

"But what about us?" interrupted Alan. "We are still part of the Like-Minded core committee, or you have dismissed us from that as well?"

"I have already tasked you to prepare the communique," replied Olive.

"It will not take much time. We will be done in an hour max," Grace joined in.

"Why don't you guys understand? For me, every minute is important, and you are asking me to wait for an hour." Olive was clearly losing her temper. She feared this meeting would follow the same trend as the previous one; everyone pointing fingers and accusing others without reaching a conclusive result.

"So you want to negotiate without us? Is there something to hide, Olive? Why are you so shady and secretive these days?" Alan asked again, paying no heed to what Olive had just said.

"For Christ's sake, there is nothing to hide, Alan. I just want to expedite the matter. Don't you get it?"

'This is not for the first…."

Olive interrupted Alan before he could complete his sentence. "Alan, I am not in the mood to explain everything. Are you interested in preparing that notification, or should I do it myself?"

"That settles it, then. It clearly shows we are not needed anymore. OK, then. Madam President, if you excuse us, we have some other pending and more important matters to look after." An angry Alan got up and left the room, followed by Grace, who fixed her stare on Olive as if to say *How dare you do that to us?*

"You shouldn't have treated them so harshly," remarked Harry.

"You too, Harry. Please tell me what I did wrong. They have been acting like angry kids and blaming me for everything," Olive replied. "Is this how mature professionals behave?"

"Forget them, Olive. Let's get down to business. What do you want us to do?" asked Paul.

Though he was posing himself as a well-wisher and someone who was concerned for Olive, deep down, Paul was happy. He was happy that Olive had lost two of her staunchest allies among the Like-Minded. With them parting their ways from Olive, it had become even easier for Paul to campaign for his candidature for the next term. He could sense that, given the circumstances, Olive's presidency would not survive for long. *It won't take much time*, he thought and smirked. The ambition to become the Club's president still burned brightly in his heart. He could visualize himself sitting in place of Olive. *With me at the helm, these kids will get to know how organizations are managed.*

"Paul, what are you thinking?"

Olive's question broke his chain of thoughts and brought him back to real life.

"Just thinking about their childish behavior. You rightly put them in their place," he replied.

The quizzical look with which Harry looked at Paul and then Olive showed his disbelief. He suspected Paul was hiding something. However, he didn't voice his concern and just shrugged his shoulders to Olive, suggesting *there was nothing to say.*

Around one o'clock in the afternoon, Sheriff showed up and joined Olive, Harry, and Paul at her office.

"Tell me, Olive, what you wanted to discuss?" he asked.

"Sheriff, you know that I want Harry to supervise the Club's internal audit. However, Rob and Ellis are objecting unnecessarily. They want Rob to co-head the audit team. This is obviously not acceptable. Hence, we will be presenting an order in the next governing body's meeting, and we want you to support us."

"OK."

"We have prepared the communique; if you want, I can share it with you."

"Sure, show me."

Olive showed him the motion they had just prepared. Going through the document alarmed Sheriff. Harry leading the audit with full authority would mean trouble for him as well. He hadn't been all that clean either in his dealings. With Rob and Joshua at his back, Sheriff had also benefitted from the opportunities that presented themselves to make some easy money. An audit of the previous three years would unearth some of his wrongdoings and could result in him going to jail, something he didn't like.

"Olive, give me some time to go through it. I will come back when done. Excuse me."

Sherrif stood up and was about to leave when Harry asked him to wait.

"It is not a report, Sheriff. Just a one-page document. You can read it here."

"Harry, have some patience," Sheriff replied smilingly.

Harry knew Sheriff well. He was sure that Sheriff would plot mischief to cover his tracks. He just knew what the sly fox Sheriff was up to but couldn't do anything because they were relying on his support to nullify Rob and Ellis' tactics.

Sheriff locked his office, put the document on his table, and called Ellis.

"Hello, Sheriff. How are you? What made you call?" Ellis couldn't believe Sheriff had called him. This was their first call in three months since he tried to coax Sheriff into voting for Rob. However, he knew one thing; Sheriff must have something very important to share.

"Hello, Ellis, guess what?"

"Tell me?"

"Olive wants to table a motion in the next governing body meeting to make Harry the leader of the audit team."

"And?"

"You know what that means?"

"Trouble," replied Ellis.

"Not just trouble, lots of trouble for all three of us," Sheriff said. "The crazy Harry will dig up everything, which may send us to jail."

"So?" gulped Ellis.

"You know, Ellis, there is a saying: You scratch my back, and I will scratch yours."

"Sheriff, you know I hate riddles. Come to the point; what do you want?"

"I think it will be in our mutual interest not to let Olive pass this bill."

"Obviously."

"But what will I get in return?" asked Sheriff.

"Your ass will be saved; what else do you want from us?" replied Ellis annoyingly. He couldn't believe Sheriff's nerves; he was bargaining even when it was clear that he would also profit from overturning the order. He was on the same ship as Rob and Ellis, yet he was negotiating for more.

"Oh, come on, Ellis; that will not be fun," Sheriff mocked displeasure.

"You are unbelievable, Sheriff. Spill it. What do you want?" Ellis almost shouted.

"Listen very carefully. I don't think this Olive's tenure can last long. In that case, I want to be welcomed back with all the privileges and with you monitoring Rob's mouth. And I want everything in writing," Sheriff lay out his demands.

"Let me check with Rob first. I will try, but I can't promise you anything at the moment," Ellis replied.

"You have one hour, Ellis. Make sure to treat me with some good news. I don't think you would want to spend your retiring years in jail."

"You may get your way this time, Sheriff, but this will not happen every time. You double-cross." Ellis disconnected the line and called Rob to update him about the matter and Sheriff's demands.

After talking to Ellis, Sheriff looked at the document and pondered to find ways to save himself from the imminent danger. He was sure that Harry would show no leniency toward anyone found guilty. Thus, he has to act quickly. Suddenly, Jacob's name flashed in his mind. *What better than a lawyer to ask for advice*, he thought and dialed the number. Sheriff shared everything with his attorney friend in one go.

"Do you have the document?" Jacob asked.

"It's in front of me," Sheriff replied.

"Send me; let me see."

"OK."

Sheriff immediately cut the line and texted a picture of the document. While waiting for Jacob's reply, Sheriff thought of all the possible scenarios available to him. At that moment, he could only think of two options: either support Olive and let Harry head the audit team or side with Rob and obstruct the bill. The former would be disastrous for him, while the latter would confirm him as a backstabber, not something a professional would want in the last years of his career. The second option was physically a less bitter pill to swallow, but has enormous social and mental ramifications. Sheriff was undecided; no, he was deprived of any feasible option. Then his cell phone rang, showing Jacob as the caller.

"Tell me, Jacob." Sheriff couldn't wait to listen to what his friend had to say.

"Sheriff, the only safe way out for you is to become the co-head of the audit team."

"And."

"As far as I know, the chief auditor has to sign the audit report and leave a note. Right?"

"Yes."

"You can write a dissenting note or something that would show that not all information or data were available during the audit. It will nullify the sole purpose of the activity, and you can't be held responsible for any wrongdoing."

Sheriff was delirious.

"Wow. Where do you get such ideas, Jacob?"

"Well, I am a lawyer, and that's my job."

"You can even prove Satan innocent, I'm sure."

"Hahaha. Proving Satan innocent is easier than saving your asses, and I have done that multiple times. Speaking of which, where is the treat, Mr Accountant?"

"You know the place; let me know whenever you are available."

"Sure will."

Sheriff couldn't believe his luck; he had just gotten out of jail. He made the changes in the draft proposed by Jacob and made his way to Olive's office. When he was about to open his door, Ellis called.

"Yes, Ellis."

"Sheriff, I just called to tell you that you are in. We accept your demands, provided you honor your commitment. Otherwise, there will be nothing between us."

"Consider it done, Ellis. I am going to Olive now. Will contact you later."

"OK."

Olive, Paul, and Harry were deliberating upon matters that needed to be taken up with Joshua when Sheriff entered.

"Hope I am not disturbing you?" he asked.

"No, no. Please, come in," Olive replied.

"Olive, I have no qualms in supporting you. However, I would want to be the co-head of the audit team."

"What does that mean? May I know the reason behind that?" asked Olive.

"Do you want me to be blunt or diplomatic?"

"Please say whatever you have to say," said Olive.

"Well, Olive, for years, Harry had opposed me and our Unionists, policies. So, you know, I am not comfortable with him as the leader of the audit team. I will just oversee the proceedings and nothing else."

"You cheat. I knew you would double-cross us someday," shouted Harry.

"Harry, please, control yourself," pleaded Olive.

"Olive, it's his trick. He wants to save himself by being a part of the team. He is no innocent guy, and he knows that" Harry was steaming.

"Sheriff, you have to trust us the way we trusted you. This audit is not against any individual, nor is it revenge. We don't harbor malicious intentions toward anyone. So, there is no need to worry about," Olive tried to show reason to Sheriff.

"Olive, you had no other choice but to take me in. Without me, you wouldn't be the president. If you want me in, please present this draft." Saying that, Sheriff handed over the paper to Olive and left the room.

"I told you, didn't I? I knew he was no one's friend. He only thinks about himself. Now look what he has done." Harry's jaw clenched as he thumbed the table, then he turned and walked out of the room.

"Harry, wait," Olive ran after him.

"What?"

"Let's discuss what we need to do; don't just leave," Olive requested.

"Do we have any other choice?" Harry asked.

Olive looked at Paul, who shook his head, suggesting no.

"Then there is nothing to discuss; just accept his condition."

Sheriff left the Club's building and then called Ellis.

"I have demanded Olive to include me as the co-lead of the audit team."

"What about us?"

"Ellis, my friend, for once, try to think with a cool head. With me in the team, you don't have to worry about anything; I will make sure all of us get a clean shit."

"How?"

Sheriff then told him about his plan.

"You are scary, Sheriff; you really are."

"You have a reason to be scared because tonight's dinner is on you. Come alone; I need to discuss something with you in person. Don't bring Rob along. I don't want his hot-headedness to mess up my plans. OK?"

"OK. Let me know when and where to come."

***

"Olive, I know you have just assumed the office, but we are expecting good news," Joshua said.

"At the moment, we are in the initial stage of the audit. So…."

"Even that is good news. At least some development is made. Otherwise, it has been in the doldrums for years."

"Yes. Sheriff and Harry are overseeing it. Up next is a fundraising event. I will be meeting with our major sponsor next week to finalize the deal. We also plan to restart publishing our newsletter. Last week, I met with our editing team responsible for the task. They were hopeful that from October, we will be up and running with our newsletter." Olive shared all the major upcoming programs.

"Why did you make Sheriff the audit lead? Harry was enough, isn't it?" Joshua asked worryingly. He sensed something was not right.

"We tried that initially, but Sheriff was apprehensive about Harry, so we included him just to quash his doubts," reasoned Olive.

"Then why not Paul?"

"He had earlier excused himself from the responsibility," informed Olive.

Joshua paused for a moment, took a few sips of his coffee, and then looked toward Olive.

"Can I meet your Like-Minded team along with Sheriff?"

"Yes, sure. When do you want it?" asked Olive.

"As soon as possible," was Joshua's reply.

"Will tomorrow do?"

"I am all yours."

"Perfect. I will plan the meeting for tomorrow and will share the schedule with you."

"OK, then, see you tomorrow," Joshua put down his empty coffee cup and got up to leave.

Chapter Nine: The Turnaround

Joshua stayed in Houston for two weeks, during which he attended a general members' meeting, a fund-raiser event, and a governing body meeting. He observed Olive's dedication and wholeheartedness toward the Club. And also how the directors were doing their utmost to make it impossible for her to perform. Not just Rob and Ellis but also her allies.

Paul was always reluctant to shoulder any major responsibility, citing family as the major excuse. His wife was undergoing treatment, so nobody could force him to give more time to the Club. However, for an experienced guy like Joshua, it was apparent that either Paul just wanted to be a free rider, availing all the privileges without performing, or had malicious intent like getting rid of Olive and becoming the president instead.

Harry, though loyal to Olive, was always in a hurry. For him, everything should happen instantly, or else he would lose hope and abandon the cause altogether. Patience and discipline required to achieve goals, either personal or combined, were traits unknown to him, and this rather immature approach was hurting his leader, Olive, more than the adversaries.

Sheriff; Joshua knew him too well and was sure he would not hesitate to obstruct Olive's path the moment he would feel his personal interests getting threatened.

Joshua could foresee Olive's fall; as per his assessment, it was just a matter of time before she would run out of her resolve and throw in the towel. The Club's internal political wrangling was crystal clear to him; he had lived long enough to differentiate when people were fighting for their ambitions and when they were raising voices for a just cause. The most disturbing point for him was that a genuine leader like Olive was fighting a losing battle, not because of her lackings but because of the rotten system that was against a young and ambitious individual. And if that person happened to be a woman, then *God save the queen!*

Joshua knew about this from his personal experience. He belonged to a well-off family; his father was a trader who was earning well enough to fulfill all the wishes of his family. Joshua had everything he could dream of. He studied in an up-scale private school, had all the cool toys, and a hefty monthly pocket money to show off in front of his friends. Being the only son of his parents, he was treated like a prince. Anderson, Joshua's father, had high hopes for his son, and they were not misplaced. Despite being an above-average student, Joshua had demonstrated great potential. He was a diamond in the rough, waiting to be polished. And who better person to polish him than his father? Consequently, when Joshua started high school, Anderson started taking him to his office to train him in all the tricks and trades of the business. He was foreseeing a bright future for his son, who would take the family business to greater heights.

However, it didn't last long. After his graduation, Joshua expressed his desire to study chartered accountancy.

"But why? Just join me and run the business. Accountancy is not easy; it will take you years." Anderson was shocked by his son's choice. He couldn't fathom that Joshua would prefer a difficult choice over a simpler life of assisting him with the business.

"Dad, that's what I want to do. Your business is good, but it is boring. It doesn't excite me," was Joshua's reply.

Knowing that chartered accountancy had gotten the better of the brightest of the students, Anderson was not convinced. Nevertheless, he half-heartedly got Joshua enrolled in an accounts college, hoping all the while that the pressure of the study would force him to quit and return to his family business sooner rather than later. It seemed he didn't know his son well enough.

Joshua excelled in college. Whatever he learned in the class, he applied in the business and managed to sort the accounts for his father. Anderson was super proud of his son, but then the big call came. As a customary requirement, Joshua joined one of the audit firms and started working as an intern. The long working hours prevented him from taking any interest in the business, which drove Anderson mad. Not long before, he confronted Joshua.

"Son, this is getting too far now. What's the point in working for others when you have your own business?"

"But, Dad, that's what I want to do."

"Enough, Joshua. Enough of this nonsense. You will resign from your firm tomorrow morning and assist me with my business. No need to serve the notice period."

"Sorry, Dad. I don't think I can do this. I haven't come this far to leave it midway." Joshua was adamant.

In a patriarchal Asian society, saying no to one's father was the cardinal sin. Anderson was incensed.

"OK, then. If you want to have it your way, then do it yourself. I am not supporting you anymore."

"Dad!" was all Joshua could say. It was hard for him to believe what he heard.

"Joshua, you need to understand that you are one of the privileged few in our country who had everything at his disposal. So why waste your time in accountancy? Come join me. After all, you are studying to get a good source of income. You already have it, then why search for it somewhere else."

"Dad, I know I am blessed, and I am thankful to you and Mom for that, but accountancy is something close to my heart. Business can come later, maybe. Don't you think I should fulfill my passion?"

"Don't try to convince with these fancy terms. You need money to progress; that's the biggest truth of life. Can your stipend support your studies? No. So why are you wasting your time? And we don't even know if you can make it. You know how many students drop out midway, right?"

"Dad, you are right about that, but at least let me try," Joshua replied. He didn't want to back down, either.

"OK, if you are passionate about something, achieve it on your own. We are done here." Saying that Anderson got up and left the dining room.

Knowing that his dad would not bulge, Joshua left the home and started living in a room with Sheriff. The stipend he was getting from the audit firm was not enough to finance his professional courses. Therefore, he started leaving out semesters to save money. This prolonged his education even further.

During his high school days, Joshua had a girlfriend named Jessica. She was an intelligent, ambitious, and confident girl. She exuded charisma, which attracted Joshua. He liked the way she used to carry herself and make herself prominent from others. Soon, they started dating. Jessica was studying psychology and loved Joshua because of his calm nature. No matter the situation, he would always remain composed, constantly finding ways to solve the problem. For Jessica, Joshua was one person in front of whom she could be herself and share all her worries, her pillar of support.

However, recently, she noticed a change in Joshua. He was clearly disturbed, and it was starting to show in his actions. She knew he had left his parent's home and was living with his friend. She was also aware of his financial situation. Therefore, one night, she decided to discuss the matter with him and, for once, swapped the supporting role with him.

"Josh, I know you are having a tough time. You can share it with me if you are comfortable."

Joshua was not accustomed to it. Usually, it was the other way around; it was he who was always encouraging others and making them feel good. Over the years, he had developed the habit of keeping his emotions to himself, buried deep inside. To him, sharing his feelings was akin to betraying himself.

Sensing that Joshua was struggling for words, Jessica got up from her chair, pulled Joshua, and hugged him hard.

"It's OK, Josh, let it go. I am here for you."

It was all he needed, and the downpour started.

"Josh, you know I have been working in a hospital. I am making enough money to support both."

"No, Jess, I don't want to burden you."

"Josh, don't you want to take this relationship further?" asked Jessica.

"Of course I do, Jess. I want to live my whole life with you."

"Ain't partners supposed to share the burden?"

"But, Jess...."

"Josh, I know this hardship is temporary; you will be able to come out of it. I just know."

"How can you be so sure?"

"Because you have the hunger and desire for perfection and are not afraid of hard work. What else is required to succeed?"

Joshua just lowered his head, thinking how much more his partner knew about him than his father. After some time, they got married and started living together. They lived on Jessica's salary while Joshua's stipend was saved for his courses. By the time Joshua completed his professional accountancy certification after three years, they had two children. Though he had been promoted to a supervisory role in the audit firm, Jessica was taking care of the majority of the expenses. Since then, he never looked back. His career took off, and eventually, he became one of the leading tax and audit consultants in his country.

Jessica's role in his life made Joshua respect women's participation in the workforce. He became more supportive and was particularly considerate about the gender pay gap and harassment. Therefore, watching Olive being forced to a wall for no fault of her own pained him. He decided to share some tips with her to confront the challenges.

"Olive, I will be leaving in a couple of days. How about having dinner together?"

"Uhh, OK."

"Bring your family along."

"Sure."

***

When Mathew and Olive reached the hotel, they found Joshua waiting for them at the table. They had dropped their kids at Mathew's parents' home. They walked to him, and Olive introduced Mathew to Joshua.

"Hello."

"Hi."

"Before anything, let's just order something; I am famished," Joshua said.

Orders were placed, and all three sat about chatting.

"I will not waste time, Olive. I have observed that not everything is well at the Club. Am I right?"

"Well, I am encountering some resistance."

"The elders are not allowing you to work, right?"

"Yes."

"Olive, let me share a story that my grandpa once told me. You know, in our country, we have walled housing societies. It happens especially in high-scale neighborhoods more because of the people's urge to create a gap between themselves and *undesirable others.* The story is from the pre-CCTV and facilities management era. People of the community used to volunteer to look after all the infrastructural requirements, some out of their social work instincts while others to be in a leadership role. In one such society, there were instances of street bulbs getting blown away. The committee—let's just call them that—used to replace the bulb to keep the street enlightened. However, they noticed that it was happening in one street only, which was at the back. When they consulted with the residents and asked them to monitor the situation, they were lackluster, and the trend continued. After some time, the committee stopped replacing the bulb, leaving the street in the dark. It created difficulties for people, but they didn't come out of their slumber. Soon, there were instances of robbery, and the residents approached the committee. They agreed to help, provided the people would ensure no bulb would be blown away in the future."

Joshua finished his story and looked at Mathew and Olive expectantly. They both seemed confused.

"What's the moral of the story?" Joshua asked.

"I don't know," Olive said blushingly.

"Olive, generally, people are lazy or scared. They don't want to challenge the status quo until it hurts them, like the residents of the street. These are the ones who can be led by anyone and anywhere. Try to help them, but don't waste much time. Secondly, there will always be miscreants. You have to be wary of such people. Then, there will be people who would want to move ahead by pulling down others, like the exhibitionists on the committee. Use them as they use you; nothing more, nothing less. Lastly, there will be people with a good heart. Identify them, help or train them, and carry them forward. They will become your biggest support.

"Always remember, Olive, whenever you will challenge status-quo, three kinds of people will join you. Those who are honest to you and your ideology, those who have a previous grudge against your opponents, and those who worship the rising run and want to make hay while it's sunshine. Honor the first group and keep the other two at a safe distance. Keep in mind they are there for you because of their own goals and will not waste a second to leave you whenever another opportunity presents itself.

"So, what do you think, Olive?"

"I believe I am getting some of the messages you are trying to convey," Olive replied.

"And they are?"

"First, I need to choose people wisely. Secondly, and more importantly, I should know when to quit. Prolonging a battle needlessly will only hurt me."

"That's it; you have got it. Perfect. Now think about it seriously."

"I will, Joshua."

Meanwhile, dinner was served, and they all enjoyed the lovely steak and seafood along with coffee.

"Talk about getting help from an unusual source," said Mathew as they drove out of the hotel parking.

"Yeah," said Olive with a self-assuring smile, which suggested she knew what she would do.

***

In the next two months, the Club's internal audit was completed. As expected, Sheriff wrote a dissenting note, citing the nonavailability of receipts and other data, nullifying the purpose of the whole exercise. He, Rob, and Ellis were happy that they had scored a major point against Olive; little did they know she was waiting for that. She had completed six months as the president and had instructed the editor to delay publishing the newsletter till the audit report. In that edition of the newsletter, Olive wrote a scathing article appraising all the members of the directors' connivance against transparency. She spared no one, not even Like-Minded directors. The article created an uproar, and Olive's phone was flooded with messages. She deliberately didn't reply to any message. Instead, she just dropped a message on the Like-Minded group, asking them to assemble in the conference room at 11 the next morning.

The other day, when Olive entered her office, she had Rob, Sheriff, and Ellis waiting for her. They barged into the room behind her.

"What's all this, Olive?" shouted Rob.

"What?" replied Olive nonchalantly as if she didn't know. Anyways, she didn't care what they were thinking.

"Your article was not in the newsletter draft we approved. Then why was it included?"

"Ohh, yeah. I asked the editor to include it later on. Sorry for not informing you."

"Do you know what it means, Olive? How can you do it without our consent?"

"I know, Rob. And let me tell you something. I am fed up with all this and am resigning."

An evil smile spread on his face.

"It took you only six months to surrender, Olive. Now you know what it means to come against us."

"I said I am resigning; didn't say I am surrendering," replied Olive swiftly.

"Isn't it the same?" asked confused Rob.

"No, and you will get to know. Now, will you excuse me?"

They left the room scratching their heads, thinking about what Olive had planned for them. She immediately wrote her resignation email and sent it to Joshua. He had been waiting for it and instantly accepted it. Then he texted Olive, "Good work; I can see you have evolved as a leader. Good luck!"

All the Like-Minded members were waiting for Olive in the conference room. As Paul entered, there was an uproar. Those loyal to Olive started shouting and abusing him for his betrayal. Harry somehow managed to soothe their emotions and asked them to wait for Olive.

"Let's hear from her, and don't jump the gun," he instructed everyone.

Olive entered the room and sensed an uneasy anxiety. The perplexed faces of the members were telling all she wanted to know; the majority was still with her. It comforted her to some degree.

"Hello, everyone. Thanks for showing up. I just wanted to inform you that I have resigned as your president. Soon, the Board will put in place an interim setup to conduct new elections."

"What," everyone gasped.

"What are you planning to do, Olive?" asked Paul.

"Getting rid of the black sheep," replied Olive.

As she said that, members booed at Paul.

Not the one to take this disrespect quietly, Paul yelled, "Are you saying I am a black sheep?"

"I didn't say any names, Paul. Why did you assume?"

"Well, your article had already said enough. There isn't much to say more," he replied.

"Did I write something wrong or unfactual?" asked Olive.

Paul was dumbfounded; he couldn't believe that Olive would confront him in front of everyone so convincingly. He got up and started toward the door.

"I want to revive our group, but I only want those who can work for the community without personal goals. I need your help. Will you support me?"

"Yes," they all roared.

"Without me, you stand no chance, Olive. The old timers will not believe you," Paul said scathingly.

"Ohh, don't worry about me, Paul. I have learned my lesson. I have gotten wiser, Paul. I have gotten wiser."

Epilogue

Shore - the ultimate descent, as we see,

Perils of power, democracy's plea.

Once-gilded halls, now shadows confide,

Deception unveiled; truth cannot hide.

Olive's unwavering, guiding light,

In the waltz of change, takes flight.

Her stance bold, justice in her gaze,

Indifference crumbles, a voice ablaze.

Amid winds of change, conflicts unfold,

Saint and sinner within, stories untold.

Moral threads woven, choices to weave,

The ultimate descent, a struggle to believe.

Olive's legacy, a beacon so bright,

In the tapestry woven, guiding light.

From deception's grasp to action's plea,

A reminder that changes begins with thee.

Acknowledgments

To the sleepless nights that kept me fueled and the food delivery person who became my muse, you've earned the spots on these pages. On my mobile device, you've seen more screen taps than a dance floor. Thanks to my procrastination for teaching me the art of writing under pressure. To my inner critic, take a sabbatical; I've got this. To all the virtual sticky notes that stuck around, this one's for you. And to the thesaurus, where would I be without you? A special nod to all those who quietly stood on the sidelines never narrated, but were always present. This book wouldn't exist without you, odd, wonderful, and slightly peculiar individuals.

This book also owes its essence to Amazon Publishing Pros' spectral partnership, particularly Afaq Ahmed and Ace White for making them the invisible quill behind my thoughts.

About the Author

Asma Jan Muhammad is an accomplished individual with a diverse range of skills and experiences. She has a strong background in finance, having received dual accountancy charters from Pakistan and, England & Wales. This educational foundation has equipped her with a deep understanding of financial management and strategic partnerships, which she has applied in her interactions with business leaders across various industries. She received recognition as one of the top 10 women CFOs in UAE - 2023, awarded by Women Entrepreneur India Magazine, recognizing her inspirational professional journey in the UAE business landscape.

Her academic achievements, including the gold medals, highlight her dedication and excellence in her field. Additionally, her commitment to community service and the recognition she has received for it showcase her passion for making a positive impact on society.

Asma's multicultural experiences in both Pakistan and the United Arab Emirates have not only enriched her perspective but have also fueled her desire to inspire others. This inspiration is evident through her writing engagements. Her book "Reflections," a compilation of motivational articles, as well as her contribution to the co-authored books "She Dares" and "She is Remarkable" by MENA Speakers, demonstrate her ability to uplift and empower others through her words.

Asma's involvement as the editor of the Pakistan Association Dubai community newsletter "Pehchaan" and her advocacy for SDG goals, especially sustainability and women-related causes with Pakistan Association Dubai, UAE, Pakistan Federation of University Women (an affiliate of Graduate Women International Switzerland) and Berkeley ME Voice of

Global Women, UAE, illustrates her dedication to contributing positively to society.

Beyond her professional and community endeavors, Asma's appreciation for the arts, including poetry, music, and playing violin, adds a creative and expressive dimension to her personality.

For those interested in learning more about Asma Jan Muhammad and her work, her online presence can be found at www.asmajanmuhammad.com. Her website likely contains additional information about her achievements, writings, and speaking engagements, providing a more comprehensive view of her inspiring journey.